Heaven and Hell

By Chuck Missler

Koinonia House

Heaven and Hell
© Copyright 2018 Koinonia House Inc.
Published by Koinonia House
P.O. Box D
Coeur d'Alene, ID 83816-0347
www.khouse.org

Author: Dr. Chuck Missler
Editor: Amy Joy

ISBN: 978-1-57821-758-8

All Rights Reserved.
No portion of this book may be reproduced in any form whatsoever without the written permission of the Publisher.

All Scripture quotations are from the King James Version of the Holy Bible.

PRINTED IN THE UNITED STATES OF AMERICA

Table of Contents

Ch. 1:	Life After Death	1
	Going to Heaven	*4*
Ch. 2:	The Physics of Immortality	11
	Body, Soul and Spirit	*14*
	Hardware and Software	*16*
	Transferring Software	*18*
Ch. 3:	Hell	21
	The Terms	*22*
	The Rich Man and Lazarus:	*26*
Ch. 4:	The Lake of Fire	31
Ch. 5:	Reincarnation and Other Errors	35
	Reincarnation	*35*
	Materialism	*37*
	Universalism	*39*
	Annihilationism	*39*
Ch. 6:	The Children	43
	Job's Children	*47*
Ch. 7:	All the People of the World	49
	Revelation 7	*51*
	Stripes	*52*
	Diligence Rewarded	*53*
	The Creation	*56*
	Written on our Hearts	*57*
Ch. 8:	The God Outside of Time	61
	Outside Time	*62*
	Quantum Entanglement	*66*
	Angels	*68*
	Stretching the Heavens	*69*
	The Word of God	*73*

Ch. 9:	At the Cross	77
Ch. 10:	Day of Judgment	81
	Two Judgements	*83*
	The Great White Throne	*84*
	Eternal Punishment	*87*
	The Bema Seat	*89*
Ch. 11:	What We Shall Be	95
	Walking Through Walls	*99*
Ch. 12:	Heaven and the New Jerusalem	103
	Marriage Supper	*105*
	The New Jerusalem	*107*
Ch. 13:	The Good News	113
Endnotes		121
About the Author		125

Chapter 1
Life After Death

What happens when we die?

This is one of those all-important questions. It's one that should keep us all awake until we know the answer. Is there life after death? Should we declare, "Eat, drink and be merry, for tomorrow we die," or do our actions in this life have repercussions in our eternities?

This subject of life after death is truly one of the toughest for many reasons. First, it's painful to get our arms around. It's a scary topic; one people love to brush away with trite clichés. Second, it has been plagued with many myths and superstition. Yet, this topic is unquestionably the most important I've ever addressed.

We like to kid around about death. A multitude of jokes begin, "An accountant/engineer/lawyer died and reached the Pearly Gates…" We find memes that say, "If I died and went to Hell, it would take me a week to realize I wasn't at work anymore." Even with all our humor about the issue, most of us understand the seriousness of the matter. If the world continues as it has, we are all going to die one day. We will all pass through that veil, and it's vital we understand what we'll face on the other side.

What happens when we die? When we pass through that portal, what's the first thing we run into? Many people deny the existence of an afterlife, but we find that even skeptics wonder as they approach that final door.

What is Heaven like?

Is there really a Hell?

We are used to the media's answers to these questions. *The Far Side* comics show God winning Jeopardy, or Satan and his cronies laughing at the notes in Hell's "suggestions" box. When Bugs Bunny and Sylvester the Cat die, they float up to a cloud with little angel wings and harps. When Bill and Ted go to Hell, they are chased by their worst nightmares, but to escape they have to beat the Grim Reaper at games of *Battleship, Clue* and *Twister*. The media have their ideas about God, Satan, Heaven and Hell.

It's interesting that the majority of American adults in our post-modern world continue to believe in life after death. Despite all the best efforts of the atheists and humanists in our universities, people generally believe that we do have souls, and they believe a final judgment does exist. According to the Pew Research Center's *2014 Religious Landscape Study*, a full 72% of Americans from all manner of backgrounds believe in some form of Heaven, defined as a place "where people who have led good lives are eternally rewarded." Fewer people are willing to believe in Hell, but 58% (nearly three-fifths) still said they believe in a place "where people who have led bad lives and die without being sorry are eternally punished."

Belief in Heaven and Hell isn't relegated to those from mainline religions. According to the Pew Research study, even among those with no particular religious viewpoint, 50% believed in a place of reward in the afterlife, and more than one-third (36%) believed in a place of punishment.

Of course, when people talk about Heaven and Hell, they have their own ideas of what those places look like. They might agree on some kind of destination of eternal punishment or reward, but their versions of the afterlife can have nothing to do with what the Bible actually says. Even among those who believe in Hell, many regard it as a symbolic place. Some believe it is simply a state of eternal separation from God's presence. Very few see Hell as an actual prison of torment and suffering where souls go after death. Fewer than one person in 100 thinks he or she will end up there.

The majority of Americans believe they will go to Heaven. There are handfuls of those who have no idea where they will go when they die, and others who believe they will return as another life form. Many people are confused and have vague mixtures of beliefs they've gleaned from a variety of religions. Another scattering of people believe they simply cease to exist after death. Their body goes into the ground, and that's it.

Going to Heaven

Let's get something straight right here at the very beginning of this book. The Bible is clear that there is both a Heaven and a Hell, and God wants everybody to go to Heaven. Did you know that? Peter and Ezekiel both tell us that God has no desire to punish us for our sins. He wants us to repent of our sins and be forgiven. That's what God wants. Listen to God's heart in the Old Testament:

> *But if the wicked will turn from all his sins that he hath committed, and keep all my statutes, and do that which is lawful and right, he shall surely live, he shall not die. All his transgressions that he hath committed, they shall not be mentioned unto him: in his righteousness that he hath done he shall live. Have I any pleasure at all that the wicked should die? saith the Lord GOD: and not that he should return from his ways, and live?*
>
> Ezekiel 18:21-23

Near the end of the Bible, an elderly Peter explains that Christ's delay in returning has been an act of mercy, giving us all more time. Jude 1:14-15 warns us that Christ's Second Coming will be a time of judgment against those who cling to ungodliness, and Peter lets us know the Lord is putting it off for our sakes.

> *The Lord is not slack concerning his promise, as some men count slackness; but is longsuffering to us-ward, not willing that any should perish, but that all should come to repentance.*
>
> 2 Peter 3:9

God wants us all to be saved. That's precisely why He sent Jesus to die for us. God sent His only begotten Son to die for the sins of the world because He loves us and wants to rescue us from our predicament. This is what Jesus tells us in the most famous passage in the entire Bible:

> *For God so loved the world, that he gave his only begotten Son, that whosoever believeth in him should not perish, but have everlasting life. For God sent not his Son into the world to condemn the world; but that the world through him might be saved.*
>
> John 3:16-17

One of the most surprising things we find in the Bible, however, is the God of Eternity does not always get what He wants. God is all-powerful, mighty and holy, but in His majesty, He has given us freedom to make our decisions, even if we reject Him.[1] There will be those who refuse to turn from their wicked ways, who refuse to humble themselves before the God of all creation. Those foolish individuals walk down our streets every day, and sin must be punished. If we do not accept Christ's death for our sins, we're stuck facing that punishment ourselves. Christ's sacrifice is the only way out of a hopeless situation. In the very next verses in John, Jesus says:

> *He that believeth on him is not condemned: but he that believeth not is condemned already, because he hath not believed in the name of the only begotten Son of God. And this is the condemnation, that light is come into the world, and men loved darkness rather than light, because their deeds were evil.*
>
> John 3:18-19

Most Americans who believe in Heaven also believe they are going there. We hope they're right, but unfortunately, many people have a completely incorrect idea about what it takes to get to Heaven. We find that a large number of people think that "being a good person" is the requirement, and that's not what the Bible says. We cannot get to Heaven by our good deeds, or by obeying the Ten Commandments, or because God loves everybody and would never send anybody to Hell. These ideas are not biblical. Turning from sin is an important part of the process (and some of us have to do it every day), but it's Christ's blood that saves us.

Certainly, God loves us. That's true. Certainly, God is not willing that anybody should perish. However, because God loves us, He gave us a way to escape our just punishment — and we have a part to play in the deal. Paul tells us plainly:

> *That if thou shalt confess with thy mouth the Lord Jesus, and shalt believe in thine heart that God hath raised him from the dead, thou shalt be saved. For with the heart man believeth unto righteousness; and with the mouth confession is made unto salvation. For the scripture saith, Whosoever believeth on him shall not be ashamed.*
>
> Romans 10:9-11

God sent His Son to make the payment for our sins, and our ticket lies in believing in Him — in repenting and believing in the work that He did on the cross for us. The work we do for Christ, we do because we love Him, and because we want to serve Him. We cannot work our way into Heaven, and woe to us if we try.

On October 21, 2003, the Barna Group released their study, *Americans Describe Their Views About Life After Death.* According to the Barna study, the Americans of the early 21st century believed in Heaven and Hell even more strongly than those in the Pew Research study a decade later. In 2003, 76% of Americans believed in some kind of Heaven, but a full 71% believed in some kind of Hell. However, even then, fewer than 1% of those interviewed believed that they themselves were heading for Hell.

The Barna study found that a large number of Americans believed they were going to Heaven, and 43% thought this was true because they had, "confessed their sins and accepted Jesus Christ as their Savior." That's nearly half, which is encouraging. However, those who recognized their need for Jesus as Savior also held a variety of contradictory beliefs. Among those who saw themselves as "born again," 10% said they believed that people are reincarnated after death, while 29% claimed it was possible to communicate with the dead, and a full 50% agreed that a person could earn their salvation based on good works.

On the other hand, we find that some self-described atheists and agnostics believe in an afterlife, and some even understand that Heaven is attained by seeking forgiveness through Jesus Christ. They might not believe Jesus is alive, or that He is God, but they understand that if God does exist after all, Jesus is the means to salvation.

It's clear that even in the United States, still considered by many to be a "Christian" country, there is a widespread problem with misinformation. Too many Americans, even those who believe in God and claim Jesus as their Savior, have failed to do their homework. They believe whatever feels most comfortable to them, according to what they like or want to believe, and not according to the Word of God.

This is an area of real concern. Whether there is a Heaven or a Hell is an important issue to get right. These are questions we can't take lightly. It's vital to be certain we know how to get to Heaven and how to avoid Hell — and we shouldn't wait until we're on death's door to consider the matter in depth. Any one of us can get hit by a truck tomorrow and have no further options.

In this little book, we will work to shed the baggage of our misconceptions and presumptions on this topic. We're going to explore what the Bible says, and we'll also consider the role of the creation and our conceptions of reality.

One of the most important things we can cover in this book is the importance of facing the truth. We have a serious problem with truth avoidance in our culture. We don't like to deal with painful or difficult realities. We'd rather watch television or hide down at the local tavern. This is a particular subject area in which willful ignorance is most dangerous, especially since it is impossible for us to remain ignorant forever. The truth will show itself to us in the end, and knowing what it is will help us ensure that it lands in our favor.

The truth has little to do with what feels good to us. It rarely has anything to do with what we'd prefer. The truth is what it is, whether we like it or not.

William Paley is credited with a well-known statement against avoiding truth. He said:

> There is a principle which is a bar against all information, Which is proof against all argument, And which cannot fail to keep

man in everlasting ignorance. That principle is condemnation before investigation.[2]

We find an equivalent idea in the writings of Solomon, who said in Proverbs 18:13: "*He that answereth a matter before he heareth it, it is folly and shame unto him.*"

In this book, I am going to suggest that we all set aside the presumptions and presuppositions that we all bring to this topic — because we all have them — and let's explore this difficult subject with the purpose of getting solid answers to hard questions.

Chapter 2
The Physics of Immortality

Frank J. Tipler is a professor of mathematical physics at Tulane University in New Orleans (and still kicking, as of this writing). He's one of these brilliant guys that's an expert in cosmology, astrophysics and information sciences. He's not a believer. He's one of these typical brilliant atheistic professors, and he undertook a project to try and reconcile what we think we know about the Big Bang.

As Tipler was working to mold two schools of thought together into one comprehensive model, he made two discoveries that shocked him. First, in the midst of trying to pull this project together, he felt he'd discovered proof of the existence of God. And not just any God, but the Judeo-Christian concept of God. (I usually quip that anybody who discovers the nature of God gets there by a miracle of the Holy Spirit, but it's an even bigger miracle if that person has a PhD.)

The second discovery Tipler made startled many people. He also now believes because of his studies in physics — not the Bible, mind you — that every human being who has ever lived will be resurrected from the dead. After he came to this conclusion, he published a book called *The Physics of Immortality*. I don't recommend the book for a number of reasons, not the least of which is that it requires an appetite for differential equations. Beyond that, we can learn a great deal more about the subject from a single chapter in 1 Corinthians. As Paul says in 1 Corinthians 15:19, "If in this life only we have hope in Christ, we are of all men most miserable." If we have eternal life through Jesus Christ, however, then we have everything. Jesus didn't promise us a trial-free time in this world. Instead, He promised us that He had conquered this world.[3]

In 1 Corinthians 15, Paul tells us that we are more than the sum of our physical body parts. I recommend that you sit down and read the entire chapter several times to appreciate the full impact of what Paul has to say. These bodies we have are temporary and corrupt, but God has eternal bodies for us, bodies meant to last forever. The eternal bodies are vastly more wonderful than these disposable bodies which we now inhabit, just as a snapdragon is vastly more beautiful than the rough little seed that died so that the flower could grow. Paul ends the chapter with a summary of the future in store for us:

> *Now this I say, brethren, that flesh and blood cannot inherit the kingdom of God; neither doth corruption inherit incorruption. Behold, I shew you a*

mystery; We shall not all sleep, but we shall all be changed, In a moment, in the twinkling of an eye, at the last trump: for the trumpet shall sound, and the dead shall be raised incorruptible, and we shall be changed. For this corruptible must put on incorruption, and this mortal must put on immortality. So when this corruptible shall have put on incorruption, and this mortal shall have put on immortality, then shall be brought to pass the saying that is written, Death is swallowed up in victory.

1 Corinthians 15:50-54

Isn't that delightful? When your back is hurting, and you find it difficult to get out of bed for the soreness in your bones and muscles, remember that this body is not the last body you'll ever have. We're all heading for an upgrade.

For a long time, materialists have assumed that reality is limited to what we can touch with our physical fingers and see with our physical eyes. The field of physics has done a lot to shatter that illusion. It is clear from quantum physics that there is more to this world than simply the four space-time dimensions we directly experience. (We will get more in depth on that subject in a few chapters.) It's important to recognize right here that there is more to us than the body we use to walk around, and most of us can sense it.

Body, Soul and Spirit

The Bible tells us that we are more than a body; we are a body, soul and spirit. The tri-fold nature of humankind pervades the Scripture from beginning to end.

The Hebrew view of humans did not partition the soul and spirit as separate fragments of our being. Instead, our soul and spirit are connected with the body to make up the human as a whole. That is, a man doesn't have a body and a soul and a spirit — he *is* a body, soul, and spirit.

The Hebrew word for "body" is *gĕviyah* (גויה) but we find it used only rarely in the Old Testament. In contrast, the word for "flesh," *basar* (בשר), is used commonly. When we do see the word "body" in the Old Testament, it's often used to indicate a corpse rather than the dwelling place for the soul. The Hebrews understood that we had a fleshly side of us, but they didn't divide the human person into separate parts. (On the other hand, the word for "body" is readily used in the Greek New Testament. The word *sōma* (σῶμα) is a familiar Greek term from which we get words like *somatic*) In the Hebrew, the body is just our hardware; it isn't the whole thing.

In Genesis we read that God formed Adam and breathed life into him:

> *And the LORD God formed man of the dust of the ground, and breathed into his nostrils the breath of life; and man became a living soul.*

Genesis 2:7

When the Old Testament speaks of a person, it often uses the word *nephesh* (נפש) the Hebrew word for "soul." In Jewish literature, the *nephesh* was understood as the invisible and immortal soul of human beings, the essence of their being.

Sometimes this word simply indicates the physical life of a person. There are occasions the word nephesh is translated "heart" or "mind" or "person." There are many times when nephesh is used to indicate the whole being, a rhetorical device called synecdoche. For instance, we might say, "twenty-five souls lost their lives in the shipwreck." Clearly, when we use the term "soul" in that manner, we mean that the whole person drowned. Ultimately, the word nephesh indicates the eternal part of us. A full 475 times out of 753 occurrences in the Old Testament it is translated as "soul" — the inner being that transcends the death of the physical body.

The word for "spirit" in the Hebrew is ruach (*ru-ach*, רוח). It has the denotation of "wind" or "breath." It is also used for the Holy Spirit and for other beings like angels or disembodied spirits, both good and bad. It's used for the seat of the emotion and the will, so there is an overlap between *ruach* and nephesh in certain usages. However, ruach is translated "wind" 92 times and "breath" another 27 times, which gives us a sense of what is intended by "spirit." Our ruach is our life force, the breath of life that animates us.

When nephesh is translated into the Septuagint, the Greek word *psyche* (ψυχή) is used 785 out of

810 times. This is the word from which we get "psychology," and it reflects a sense of the mind or the heart — the inner man. It is clearly seen as the immortal soul rather than just the life force. The word ruach, on the other hand, is translated into Greek as *pneuma* (πνεῦμα) the word from which we get "pneumatic," reflecting the connection to breath, wind, or air. It's a breath from the nostrils. In the Greek, it's the spirit, the vital principle by which the body is *alive*. Again, it's also the name given to the third Person of the Trinity — the Holy Spirit.

Hardware and Software

As we consider these things, I see them through the eyes of a technology addict. I think we are, in many respects, much like computers. If I were to build a computer, I would know everything there is to know about every piece of hardware inside that machine. It would have a central processing unit, a CPU where the central electronics manipulates information according to a computer language. It would have memory. There would be electronics involved that would permit input and output, generally involving a keyboard and a mouse. I could carefully solder in every microcircuit, every transistor, every capacitor for that computer and know it inside and out. Yet, if I did this, I still wouldn't be able to foresee the computer's behavior — because that would be determined by the software that someone eventually installed on it.

In the early days, computers were just complex adding machines that ran programs. These days, we have computers that can alter their own memories. They have programs that allow them to learn. This ability to modify their own programs is what differentiates these computers from powerful calculators.

Consider the architecture of software. In software, we primarily find a master program — the operating system that manages the computer for us. Inside the operating system we find a super program that manages memory. We don't know where files are physically located, but we can pull them up through the memory management system in which several application programs can be running simultaneously. The operating system includes a user interface which makes the computer readily usable even for those who have no experience in computer programming. Microsoft has long given us "Windows" which allows us to look at different programs in their own visual boxes. Mac computers have included a menu bar since 1984. Different operating systems (OS) offer different user interfaces, and users can choose the OS that best suits their needs.

When new software is placed on the computer, it can't be discerned by x-raying the computer. There's nothing on the outside that tells us what the software contains. We simply know how the software makes the computer behave. Yet, if that computer hardware were to fail, we would not have to lose the software. We could copy the software and move it onto another device, and those same programs could run just like they always have.

The hardware is no good without software, because it needs that programming in order to operate. The software is no good without hardware, because it needs something on which to run. Even then, the hardware and the software are no good unless the computer is plugged in. Only when electricity is available do the hardware and the software work together to run programs.

What does all this have to do with us?

I think we human beings have many of the same characteristics as computers. The being that people see when they look at you or me, is not the most important part of us. They can see our hardware. They can see our temporary residence, and if they put us on a surgical table they might see all our inner circuitry. However, if our hardware has no electricity running through it, it's just dead bits of plastic and metal and wiring.

I suggest that the most important part of us is our software. Once our hardware breaks down, there's an eternal part of us that can be moved. The real us isn't physical and it isn't temporary. The real us is the software inside a temporary dwelling.

Transferring Software

I had an interesting experience a few years ago. Back when I was traveling a lot, I depended greatly on my laptop. It gave me the freedom to get my writing done while I jetted about from one engagement to another. After using it for several years, it died on me, which caused me no small grief. I took it to the shop to get it fixed, but they told me it was a lost cause. I couldn't afford to buy a new one. I didn't know what to do. Thankfully, some Christian friends came to my rescue and gave me a new laptop with all the bells and whistles. I was more grateful for this than I can tell you.

I'll never forget the day I fired up that new laptop for the first time. I was able to load it with all the software that I had collected over the course of 20 years, and I was back in familiar territory. All the files I needed were there for me to use, except that they ran about a hundred times faster than they had before.

That experience left an impression on me, and I want to share with you my *aha* moment: you and I are heading for an upgrade. Software has no mass. If I take a thumb drive and fill it with 10 gigabytes of information, it weighs no more than it did brand new. The real us has no mass. This means that our software is not affected by time. One day this slow and tired piece of hardware in which we live will boot up for the last time. The part of us that is eternal will be transferred to a new body that is beyond anything we can imagine.

I can take this analogy even a little farther.

If I buy a program, I can learn very little about its internal programming by how it's running. I only can observe how it causes my computer to behave. The only way I can find out about how the software's organized is to get the programmer's manual. The same is true with you and me. This is the reason the field of psychology is doomed to frustration; it's attempting to understand our architecture from our external behavior. We have to get the programmer's guide in order to understand the nuts and bolts of our software.

We are a body, soul and spirit. When we die physically, the body is separated from the soul. However, software doesn't function as it's meant to function without a CPU to run the programs. We have a new body in store for us, one that will never break down or short circuit. You and I are eternal, whether we like it or not. That's good news for those who are saved, but it's terrible news if we're not.

We are destined for a resurrection. What then? What comes next?

Chapter 3
Hell

If the Lord tarries, we will all die one day. Every one of us. The soul will be united with another body at the resurrection. The big question we all have to ask is, what happens then? Is there really a Hell? What will Heaven be like? Most importantly, how do we prepare ourselves for eternity?

Let's start with the scary one. Let's look at what the Bible says about Hell.

There is clear warning in the Scripture of our need to "flee from the wrath to come."[4] However, pastors no longer like to speak of Hell, and people tend to avoid the matter like they do brambles or burnt broccoli. Fire and brimstone preaching is out of style, and Hell is a touchy, unpleasant subject. We don't like to think about it, let alone talk about it, even in Christian circles. Because of this indifference, there's widespread ignorance on the whole topic, and because of the ignorance, we have doubts about the reality of Hell.

Many Christians don't want to believe in Hell. There's a lot of denial, so it has become an irritating subject. People are happier dismissing the threat, which leads to even greater ignorance. This is a tragic cycle that we have within the body of Christ.

We don't want to deal with the full justice of God, and so we leave people out there exposed. We don't want to believe the hurricane is coming, so we fail to tell people to get inside for safety.

We have pictures in our head of Hell based on silly movies and cartoons. Gary Larson always presents Hell as a place of fire and torture in *The Far Side*. His comics are clever and entertaining, but he also shows Satan as the guy in charge of Hell. Most popular literature has this common misconception. Satan does not rule in Hell. Hell was created as Satan's place of incarceration.

We use the term "Hell" loosely today without understanding what it is and what it means to go there. Teenage boys will foolishly talk about hanging out in Hell with each other. They believe that's the place they belong, but they have no real fear of Hell or a desire to escape it. They have accepted the idea that Heaven is boring, and they think that they'll be able to rock out in Hell. This is also the fault of popular misconceptions. Heaven will not be boring, and there will be no sense of companionship in Hell.

The Terms

The word "hell" itself comes from the Saxon word *helen* which means "to cover." Hell is the covered place, the invisible place. However, in the Bible there are a number of words translated "Hell," each with its own particular nuance. This can get confusing. We will go through each of these terms to clarify them.

Sheol is the Hebrew word for the place of the dead. The word is derived from a term meaning "to ask" or "to demand," indicating that death is never satisfied. The word is used in the Old Testament sixty-five times. Sheol is translated as "Hell" about half the time, but it's also commonly translated as "grave." This is not a precise rendition, because the grave is simply a hole in the ground where a dead person is buried. There can be many graves, but Sheol is always used in the singular. Sheol is the place "downward" — the habitation of the disembodied spirits, rather than just the *qeber*, the ground where dead bodies are placed. Proverbs 21:16 calls Sheol the "congregation of the dead." It is the abode for the souls of both the Old Testament wicked and righteous who have passed away. It is described in Job 17:16 as deep and dark, with prison bars, and the dead go down to it.

The first place the term Sheol is mentioned in the Bible is in Genesis 37:35 when Jacob is confronted with the apparent death of Joseph. Jacob's older sons bring him Joseph's beautiful coat covered in blood, and Jacob is convinced that Joseph has been killed. He grieves greatly, and his children all try to comfort him, but he won't be comforted. He declares that he will go down into Sheol "unto my son" mourning. It seems that Jacob assumes his son was still conscious after death. Jacob doesn't think Joseph has been buried, because the lad was presumably eaten by animals. Even so, Jacob takes for granted that he will ultimately be united with Joseph when they are both dead.

Jacob also says he will go *down* to Sheol. We find that the Hebrew word Sheol, as the Greek word Hades, is a geocentric concept. There is this idea that the place of the dead is down in the center of the earth. That's not necessarily literal, but it's certainly the way it was viewed idiomatically. Sheol is under the earth, or in the lower parts of the earth all throughout the Scripture.

Qeber / kever is the Hebrew word for the grave. This is a place of physical burial. We know that this term is not synonymous with Sheol, because every time that Sheol is translated in the Greek Septuagint, the word *Hades* is used rather than the Greek word *mnemeion*. Mnemeion is the word used for a tomb or a sepulcher — a place of remembrance. In the Septuagint, there is no confusion about this like there is in the King James' rendering of these terms. The Greek-speaking Jews in Alexandria who translated the Old Testament into Greek always translated Sheol as Hades and never as mnemeion. It is the Hebrew word *kever* that is translated as "grave." Also remember that in those early days, sepulchers were often in caves rather than in the ground. Abraham bought a field with a cave in Mamre in Canaan as a *kever*, as a burying place, and his family members were buried there for generations.[5] In other words, Sheol and kever are not even in the same location in the ground.

Kever has to do with burial, and it can be pluralized. Sheol is never pluralized; there is only one Sheol. The grave is accessible before and after death, but interment in a grave is not necessary for an individual to go to Sheol. A grave can be purchased or sold and is treated as personal property. Sheol is never spoken as being bought or sold, and it is not owned by any man. Bodies in the grave are unconscious, but those in Sheol are conscious. We will see several instances of this.

Hades is the classic Greek word for the place of the dead. The very word brings to mind the Greek god of the lower regions. Hades' Roman equivalent was Pluto, although in Roman mythology we also find Orcus, the god of the netherworld and punisher of those who swear false oaths. Hades is translated ten times as "Hell" in the New Testament. In biblical Greek, Hades is the very depths of the earth, the common receptacle of disembodied spirits of every kind. Hades is divided into two separate locations in the Greek understanding: Elysium and Tartarus. Elysium is the equivalent of paradise, while Tartarus is the dark place of punishment.

In the Bible, Hades refers to the abode of the unsaved dead prior to the Judgment, as described in Revelation 20. It is equivalent to Sheol. It is a prison with gates[6] and bars[7] and chains.[8]

The Rich Man and Lazarus:

In Luke 16, Jesus tells a story about a poor man and a rich man who both die. The rich man goes to Hades, where he is tormented by flames of fire, while the poor man is carried by the angels to "Abraham's bosom" where he is comforted. When Jesus tells parables, He doesn't offer us names for the characters involved. This story is different; it is told as though it's a true series of events. Jesus gives us the name of the poor beggar in this story. His name is Lazarus, and we get a sense that what Jesus is describing actually happened to real individuals.

> *There was a certain rich man, which was clothed in purple and fine linen, and fared sumptuously every day: And there was a certain beggar named Lazarus, which was laid at his gate, full of sores, And desiring to be fed with the crumbs which fell from the rich man's table: moreover the dogs came and licked his sores.*

Luke 16:19-21

That's the background. The words that Jesus Himself speaks here provide us with what I believe is the most reliable understanding of what happened to Old Testament persons when they died. Most of the early church fathers regarded paradise as a part of Heaven, not Hades, and the two-compartment view is somewhat an accommodation to the Greek conception, but it is one that undergirds the Lord's teaching in Luke 16.

> *And it came to pass, that the beggar died, and was carried by the angels into Abraham's bosom: the rich man also died, and was buried; And in hell he lift up his eyes, being in torments, and seeth Abraham afar off, and Lazarus in his bosom.*
>
> Luke 16:22-23

This is interesting. Somehow the happiness and comfort of Lazarus isn't hidden from the once-rich man. Whether he literally sees Lazarus or is simply conscious of the fact, the man in Hades/Sheol recognizes that Lazarus is in Abraham's bosom. He is conscious. He is aware of his predicament, and yet even in this place of terrible suffering, he can see across the great chasm and speak to Abraham.

> *And he cried and said, Father Abraham, have mercy on me, and send Lazarus, that he may dip the tip of his finger in water, and cool my tongue; for I am tormented in this flame.*
>
> Luke 16:24

We find a fire theme here. We see that the man in Hades feels things. He is tormented and longs for water, but he is also able to speak to Abraham. He begs Abraham, and obviously Abraham can hear him because he replies to the tormented man. The rich man sees that Lazarus is there with Abraham, and he wants Abraham to give Lazarus a little errand — just a small errand on his behalf.

> *But Abraham said, Son, remember that thou in thy lifetime receivedst thy good things, and likewise Lazarus evil things: but now he is comforted, and thou art tormented. And beside all this, between us and you there is a great gulf fixed: so that they which would pass from hence to you cannot; neither can they pass to us, that would come from thence.*
>
> Luke 16:25-26

There's no fixing the situation. There's no helping the man in Hades. They can speak to each other across the chasm, but they cannot reach out to each other. Abraham acknowledges what they both know — that the man in Hades is getting what he deserves. Yet, the man wants to protect others from ending up there in Hades with him. Since he can't save himself, he desires to save his brothers:

> *Then he said, I pray thee therefore, father, that thou wouldest send him to my father's house: For I have five brethren; that he may testify unto them, lest they also come into this place of torment. Abraham saith unto him, They have Moses and the*

*prophets; let them hear them. And he said,
Nay, father Abraham: but if one went
unto them from the dead, they will repent.
And he said unto him, If they hear not
Moses and the prophets, neither will
they be persuaded, though one rose from
the dead.*

Luke 16:27-31

Notice that the tormented man doesn't complain about injustice. He never questions the fixity of his eternal destiny. He knows he deserves what he is experiencing. At the same time, he is able to feel concern about his brothers. They're on his heart, and he wants to find a way to help them avoid the same awful fate he's experiencing. He begs Abraham to send Lazarus to those brothers to get them to repent, because he recognizes that if they listen to Lazarus and repent, they can be rescued from the punishment he's living. Abraham tells him it's no use. They won't listen to Lazarus even if he rises from the dead.

Of course, One far greater than Lazarus did rise from the dead — Jesus Christ, the Son of God. Yet, those who won't listen to Moses and the prophets also won't listen to Jesus, because those prophets spoke of Him.

There is a sobering understanding that we can all draw from this. That once-rich man who asked for a touch of water is still longing for it today. The final judgment is still in the future, and those in Hades remain there until that day.

In Revelation, John told us that a day is coming when every being who ever lived is brought before God for judgment, saying:

> *And the sea gave up the dead which were in it; and death and hell delivered up the dead which were in them: and they were judged every man according to their works. And death and hell were cast into the lake of fire. This is the second death. And whosoever was not found written in the book of life was cast into the lake of fire.*
>
> Revelation 20:13-15

Chapter 4
The Lake of Fire

There is another term that is distinct from Hades, and while Hades is destroyed, this place will not be.

Gehenna is a term that Jesus uses. It's also translated "Hell" in the Bible, but it's distinct from the underworld of Hades. Hades is temporary, while Gehenna is forever. Gehenna is in eternity. Everything that's in Hades will ultimately end up being thrown into Gehenna, as John tells us in Revelation 20. Gehenna has no end; it's outside the time dimension.

The word Gehenna originally referred to *Gai Ben-Hinnom* — the Valley of the Son of Hinnom. We learn in Jeremiah that idolatrous Jews once offered their children in sacrifice to the god Molech in that valley.[9] In later years, Gehenna became the city dump, where garbage constantly burned. They dumped not only their trash there, but dead animals and filth. The Kidron Valley is situated on the east of Jerusalem between the city and the Mount of Olives, and the Tyropoean Valley is on the west. Gehenna is a deep, narrow ravine on the south side of Jerusalem, and it once served as the city dump. Jesus uses this place of perpetual burning idiomatically as a reference to Hell. It's a place of constant fire, and ultimately it refers to the lake that burns with fire and brimstone.

There are twelve occurrences of the word Gehenna in the New Testament. In eleven of those twelve occurrences, the Lord uses it as an idiom for the ultimate destiny of the unsaved. The unsaved are temporarily held in Hades/Sheol, but they will meet their eternal destiny in the lake of fire and brimstone.

The Beast and False Prophet are thrown into Gehenna in Revelation 19:20. We reach a great climax in Revelation 20:14, however, when Death and Hades are themselves cast into the brimstone lake. Even Hades is temporary. It's destined to be cast into the lake of fire, which is the second and final death.

It's important to understand some things about Gehenna. It was not created for human beings. It was specifically prepared as the destiny of Satan and his angels:

> *Then shall he say also unto them on the left hand, Depart from me, ye cursed, into everlasting fire, prepared for the devil and his angels:*
>
> Matthew 25:41

There is no good reason for humans to end up in Gehenna. Jesus died for the sins of all the people that have ever existed. Those who are thrown into Gehenna are those who have disregarded God's provision to rescue them from their eternal punishment. It's the greatest tragedy of all time that people for whom Christ died will lose their opportunity to spend eternity with Him.

The *phrear abussos*, the abyss, is clearly the bottomless pit. In Revelation 20:3, Satan is imprisoned in the abyss for 1000 years. He's released at the end of the Millennium for a short time, but in the meanwhile the earth enjoys a period of rest without his victimizations. Earlier, in Revelation 11:7 and 17:8, the Beast emerged from this pit, and in chapter 9, the demon locusts exploded out of it. Job refers to *shachath* — "the pit" — as a place of destruction for the unredeemed.[10]

The New Testament writers used the term Hades, but they also used the Greek term *Tartarus*. The King James translates Tartarus as "Hell" without any distinction, but in Homer's *Iliad*, Tartarus is the deepest abyss of Hades, as far below Hades as the earth is below Heaven. It's possible that Tartarus is equivalent to the bottomless pit. Tartarus is a Greek concept, but Peter makes use of this term to describe the punishment of fallen angels, echoing Jude 1:6.

> *For if God spared not the angels that sinned, but cast them down to hell, and delivered them into chains of darkness, to be reserved unto judgment...*

2 Peter 2:4

The idea of a "lowest Hell" can be found in the Old Testament. David in Psalm 86:13 says, "For great is thy mercy toward me; and thou hast delivered my soul from the lowest Hell." There, the word is Sheol, but the idea that there can be a lowest part of Sheol is noteworthy.

In no place, whether Hades or Tartarus or the Abyss, does Satan rule. Satan does not hold authority over Gehenna. It was prepared as a place of punishment for him.

Satan is condemned, and he knows it. Revelation 12:12 tells us he's come down to the earth in great wrath, because he knows his time is short. He is not like the rich man who wanted to warn his brothers; Satan intends to drag as many down with him as he can. His desire is to deceive and corrupt and to turn people away from God. Any false idea or lie about God had its origin in Satan's passion to destroy people for whom Christ died.

Chapter 5
Reincarnation and Other Errors

There are a lot of bad ideas out there. I often run into the issue of reincarnation around Halloween. When I do, I love to call attention to a poem by the old curmudgeon cowboy Wallace McRae:[11]

Reincarnation
"What does Reincarnation mean?"
A cowpoke asked his friend.
His pal replied, "It happens when
Yer life has reached its end.
They comb yer hair, and warsh yer neck,
And clean yer fingernails,
And lay you in a padded box
Away from life's travails."

"The box and you goes in a hole,
That's been dug into the ground.
Reincarnation starts in when
Yore planted 'neath a mound.
Them clods melt down, just like yer box,
And you who is inside.
And then yore just beginnin' on
Yer transformation ride."

"In a while, the grass'll grow
Upon yer rendered mound.
Till some day on yer moldered grave
A lonely flower is found.
And say a hoss should wander by
And graze upon this flower
That once wuz you, but now's become
Yer vegetative bower."

"The posy that the hoss done ate
Up, with his other feed,
Makes bone, and fat, and muscle
Essential to the steed,
But some is left that he can't use
And so it passes through,
And finally lays upon the ground
This thing, that once wuz you."

"Then say, by chance, I wanders by
And sees this upon the ground,
And I ponders, and I wonders at,
This object that I found.
I thinks of reincarnation,
Of life and death, and such,
And come away concludin': 'Slim,
You ain't changed, all that much.'"

I enjoy that poem, and I present it to you as a bit of tongue-in-cheek humor. However, there are a number of people who take reincarnation seriously and may not realize that it's not a biblical concept. People embrace the idea of reincarnation for a variety of reasons, one of which is the hope that we have more than one chance to get it right.

It's important to realize that there is nothing in the Bible about reincarnation. Hebrews 9:27 states clearly, "*And as it is appointed unto men once to die, but after this the judgment:*" There are no second and third and twentieth chances to "get it right." This is it. This is our one go at life. Belief in reincarnation offers a false hope. It might seem harmless enough, but those who believe in reincarnation might not recognize they need to seek God and be saved. We are all in trouble unless we repent and seek God's forgiveness, and that makes any kind of deceptive idea extremely dangerous. People are perishing for lack of knowledge![12]

The Bible's answer to the problem of our sin is the atonement of Christ. We are born with a sin nature, and we continually fail to obey God, but our sins are paid for by Christ. His sacrifice is sufficient. This is the primary theme of the Bible from Genesis 1 to Revelation 22, and it undercuts any theory of reincarnation or transmigration of the soul.

People have contrived reasons to disbelieve all throughout human history. They simply don't like God's way of handling things, and so they come up with ideas of their own.

Materialism

Materialism is one form of disbelief that is popular in our culture today, especially among scientists. Science requires experimentation that can make predictions and get the same result every time. It also will not allow God as an answer to questions, because God doesn't fit into a test tube very well. God has said, "Do not test me."[13] Many people have made the mistake of concluding that since the spiritual world cannot be directly tested, it does not exist. They believe that the *real* world is the material world, the tangible world we can grab and taste and smell. However, materialists are misinformed. We'll deal with this more in a later chapter, because the discoveries of modern physics point to a much greater reality beyond the four space-time dimensions we see and touch directly.

Obviously, if there is no spiritual world, then there is no need to worry about eternal punishment or reward. Materialists believe we cease to exist when we die. We are buried and the worms eat us, and that's it. The best thing we can do to live forever is to make an impact on the world we leave behind. It's a bonus if people continue to talk about us or read our books or watch our movies or repeat our speeches after we're gone.

Materialism is a terrible error, however, because the spiritual world is there. God *is*. That's what the name Yahweh means, in fact: "I AM." There is a great deal of evidence to support the existence of the spiritual realm, and many materialists have simply failed to do their homework where spiritual things are concerned. They will have a rude surprise when they die and find that it isn't the end, and they didn't cease to exist after all.

Universalism

Universalism is the pleasant idea that we all eventually arrive safely in Heaven. It says there might be various ways of reaching Heaven, and we might take different routes, but all souls go to Heaven in the end. That is not what the Bible teaches.

We find in Revelation 20:10 that the Beast and the False Prophet are still in the lake of fire and brimstone, where they've been since the beginning of the Millennium. After the Millennium, the devil is thrown in with them, and they "*shall be tormented day and night for ever and ever.*" A few verses later, death and Hell are thrown into the lake of fire as well. Finally, in Revelation 20:15 they are followed by all who are not found written in the Book of Life.

The idea of universalism is appealing but we do not find it in the Bible. However, we do know one important thing: Jesus Christ is a righteous judge. The Lord does not judge by outward appearances, and He knows every human being inside and out.[14] We can take comfort in the understanding that He will judge wisely and righteously.

Annihilationism

There are those who hope the souls of the wicked are simply obliterated, that they cease to exist at all. That is, some people choose to believe that once the soul goes to Hell, it is ultimately destroyed forever. The verse that many use to support this position is Matthew 10:28, which says:

> *And fear not them which kill the body, but are not able to kill the soul: but rather fear him which is able to destroy both soul and body in hell.*

The Greek word "destroy" here is *apollumi*, which we recognize as the root of Apollyon, "the destroyer" the angel of the bottomless pit found in Revelation 9:11. While the word does mean "to destroy" it doesn't mean to annihilate. It's more along the lines of destroying somebody's career — crushed and ruined forever.

Throughout the Bible, verses contradict the idea of annihilation. In Matthew 25:46, Jesus warns that the wicked "*shall go away into everlasting punishment: but the righteous into life eternal.*" The word for both "everlasting" and "eternal" in this verse are the same Greek word, *aionios*. It means "perpetual" with the sense of forever. It's the same word for eternal punishment and eternal life. We can't escape the linkage.

It's the same in the Old Testament. In Daniel 12, an angel of God gives Daniel a brief overview of the end of times, saying:

> *And many of them that sleep in the dust of the earth shall awake, some to everlasting life, and some to shame and everlasting contempt. And they that be wise shall shine as the brightness of the firmament; and they that turn many to righteousness as the stars for ever and ever.*

Daniel 12:2-3

The word "everlasting" here is *olam*, which indicates perpetuity, always, or eternity. Some will awaken to everlasting life, and some to everlasting shame. It's forever either way.

In Revelation 14, we find that taking the Mark of the Beast is cause for eternal punishment. An angel announces with a loud voice:

> *And the third angel followed them, saying with a loud voice, If any man worship the beast and his image, and receive his mark in his forehead, or in his hand, The same shall drink of the wine of the wrath of God, which is poured out without mixture into the cup of his indignation; and he shall be tormented with fire and brimstone in the presence of the holy angels, and in the presence of the Lamb: And the smoke*

> *of their torment ascendeth up for ever and ever: and they have no rest day nor night, who worship the beast and his image, and whosoever receiveth the mark of his name.*
>
> Revelation 14:9-11

We have all been duly warned. There is nothing temporary about this. This is serious language.

My biggest concern is for those who doubt they will go to Hell. Nearly three out of every five Americans believes in an eternal place of punishment, but hardly anybody worries that they might go there. Nobody wants to talk about Hell. Nobody likes the thought of it. This is dangerous and tragic, especially since Jesus Christ spoke more about Hell than He did about Heaven. Jesus, the very Creator of the universe,[15] became a human being to suffer the brutal death of the Cross in order to save us from the danger of eternal punishment in Hell. We need to face up to the facts about Hell right now before it's too late.

Chapter 6
The Children

But, what about children?

Many of us are concerned about children who die without knowing Christ, and I get a lot of questions about them. Whenever this issue comes up, I think of David's child in 2 Samuel 12.

David's first son by Bathsheba was ill, and David prayed and fasted hoping God would change His mind and allow the child to live. David refused to eat. He refused to get off the ground. When the child died, the servants were afraid to tell David for fear of what he would do to himself. As soon as he heard the news, though, David cleaned himself up and went back to work. His servants were shocked. Read what David said to them.

> *Then said his servants unto him, What thing is this that thou hast done? thou didst fast and weep for the child, while it was alive; but when the child was dead, thou didst rise and eat bread. And he said, While the child was yet alive, I fasted and wept: for I said, Who can tell whether GOD will be gracious to me, that the child may live? But now he is dead, wherefore*

should I fast? can I bring him back again?
I shall go to him, but he shall not return
to me.

2 Samuel 12:21-23

David knew he would eventually join his son, who was just a baby.

Children are subject to death just as we are, and they are born with the same sin infection that we all have. However, I have all confidence that their accountability is waved, and Christ's blood covers them without discrimination.

Paul says something interesting in Romans 7:9 that I think is connected to this: "For I was alive without the law once: but when the commandment came, sin revived, and I died." When I analyze this, I conclude the only time that Paul could have been alive without the law was before the age of accountability. He was apparently saved when he was at a tender age, because he wasn't regarded as having the law.

We find a most interesting passage in 1 Kings regarding the death of a child. God has declared war against the house of Jeroboam I because he has led Israel into idolatry. Jeroboam's son Abijah falls ill, and Jeroboam sends his wife to Ahijah the prophet to find out what will happen to the boy. As soon as she arrives, Ahijah tells her that God is going to put to death all of Jeroboam's offspring, and they will die in terrible ways because of the family sin. However, God is going to have mercy on Jeroboam's son Abijah, because his heart is pleasing to God. The child will still die, but in a way that has honor and love associated with it:

> *Arise thou therefore, get thee to thine own house: and when thy feet enter into the city, the child shall die. And all Israel shall mourn for him, and bury him: for he only of Jeroboam shall come to the grave, because in him there is found some good thing toward the LORD God of Israel in the house of Jeroboam.*
>
> 1 Kings 14:12-13

It's a tragic story, but it can make us imagine little Abijah in his father's house. He probably didn't know much about God at all. He was surrounded by idolatry, yet he still had a good heart toward God — and God saw him and honored him for it.

It's clear that Jesus had a heart for children. Consider some of the things He tells His disciples:

> *Take heed that ye despise not one of these little ones; for I say unto you, That in heaven their angels do always behold the face of my Father which is in heaven.*
>
> Matthew 18:10

> *And they brought young children to him, that he should touch them: and his disciples rebuked those that brought them. But when Jesus saw it, he was much displeased, and said unto them, Suffer the*

little children to come unto me, and forbid them not: for of such is the kingdom of God.

Matthew 10:13-14

And Jesus called a little child unto him, and set him in the midst of them, And said, Verily I say unto you, Except ye be converted, and become as little children, ye shall not enter into the kingdom of heaven. Whosoever therefore shall humble himself as this little child, the same is greatest in the kingdom of heaven.

Matthew 18:2-4

As we consider these things, we need to remember the heart of God. God loved us first, and children are precious to Him.

What *is* the age of accountability? I suspect that it's different for each child, based on their own awareness of the world and their ability to know anything about God and recognize their own sin. Most children just want to be loved, and Jesus loves them. We know that people who give their lives to the Lord as children are far more likely to stay with Him their whole lives than those who never hear about him.

Children's ministries are incredibly important. We all need to support our local children's ministries and missions and Christian summer camps — any outreach that helps children know Christ while they are still young. We also need to show Christ's love to the children in our lives. There are plenty of troubled kids out there that could use some longsuffering love from people in the Christian community. "You matter to me. You matter to Jesus." That's our responsibility.

Job's Children

I want to share something I found in the book of Job that I believe most people overlook. Remember, Job had 10 children. They were grown, and Job 1:5 tells us Job made sacrifices for them daily, because he was concerned for the states of their souls:

> *There was a man in the land of Uz, whose name was Job; and that man was perfect and upright, and one that feared God, and eschewed evil. And there were born unto him seven sons and three daughters.*
>
> Job 1:1-2

Job had huge holdings, vast numbers of sheep, camels, oxen and donkeys and a huge household; and verse three tells us he was the greatest man in the east. We all know the story. Satan is allowed to take everything from Job — his possessions, his health, and his 10 children. Job spends much of the book suffering and trying to defend himself from the critical suggestions of his so-called friends. In the end, however, God restores all of Job's belongings. In fact, He gives Job twice the numbers of sheep, oxen, camels and donkeys than he had at the beginning. He also gives him seven more sons and three more daughters.

This is interesting. The LORD gives Job twice as much livestock as he had before, but He does not give him twice as many children. Job only receives the same number of children that he had before. That doesn't seem right. At first, I felt that Job got short-changed a bit. Then I realized there's a significant difference between Job's belongings and his children. He didn't completely lose the seven sons and three daughters who died. They're waiting for him. When God gave Job ten additional sons and daughters, it's counted as double because he will get to see his first children again.

I know what it means to have a child die suddenly and unexpectedly. I have lost two sons, one quite recently. Those who have had their children die know the incredible pain of it, but we have a Comforter who understands. God knows all about losing sons too.

Chapter 7
All the People of the World

It's easy to understand that God will take in His arms the children who die, but what about all those people in the jungles or remote places of the earth who have never heard the Gospel? What about those people raised in pagan cultures who don't know any better? Surely, God won't toss people in the lake of fire if they haven't even heard about Jesus.

The Bible gives us clues about these things as well.

First, we need to realize something important. As concerned as we might be about the people in pagan cultures, God knows them and loves them far better than we do. God cares more about the aged Dalit on the streets of Mumbai and the little children in Bangkok than any one of us cares about *anything*. We ask the question, "What about them?" but it's embarrassing how little we even think about the lost people around the globe. When we assume God plans to send certain people to Hell, do we even think to pray for them? Do we pray for the missionaries reaching out to them? Do we donate to missions? We need to value the people in Eritrea and Niger and Estonia, Laos and Detroit, because Jesus died for them. If they have been raised in a culture of lies and deceit, shouldn't we be praying for the work of the Holy Spirit in their lives? Shouldn't we be seeking their salvation?

Before we assume that God has abandoned any people groups, I want to point to a little story.

Amy Carmichael was a missionary to India for 55 years during the late 19th and early 20th century. She opened an orphanage and a mission in the southern town of Dohnavur, and she is famous for rescuing little girls from sexual slavery as temple prostitutes. Miss Carmichael wrote many books, one of which was about an Indian woman named Mimosa.[16]

When Mimosa was just a little girl, she heard about the God of love for just a few short minutes. Mimosa didn't even get a chance to hear about Jesus and the plan for salvation before her father took her away. She only knew that there was a God who loved her. That was it. For the next decades of her life, that God of love was there for little Mimosa. Surrounded by Hindus who disapproved of her, with no human support system, Mimosa pressed on, trusting in her God. Through the birth of her sons and the death of one, through years of poverty and want, God took care of Mimosa. It's a precious story, because it shows the working of God's kindness, even in the darkness of the pagan world.

Miss Carmichael was only able to write down Mimosa's story because that dear woman finally made her way back to the mission as an adult woman with a passel of sons. It makes us wonder how many children of God are trusting in His love in the darkest, most troubling places in the world, where we never get a chance to hear about them.

If this issue concerns us deeply, the Bible says several things that I think we can take to heart.

Revelation 7

First, we know that there will be people in Heaven from all tribes and tongues and nations in the world. We know this, because John plainly tells us so. In Revelation, he describes an innumerable multitude of people from all around the world standing before God's throne, clothed in white:

> *After this I beheld, and, lo, a great multitude, which no man could number, of all nations, and kindreds, and people, and tongues, stood before the throne, and before the Lamb, clothed with white robes, and palms in their hands; And cried with a loud voice, saying, Salvation to our God which sitteth upon the throne, and unto the Lamb*
>
> Revelation 7:9-10

This list of "all nations, and kindreds, and people, and tongues" doesn't seem to leave out any people group. Think of the countries that have fifty dialects among the different villages; some of the people from all those dialects will be in Heaven. We can trust that God will provide His witness to them in some way or another.

We see throughout the Bible that God cares about all the people of the world. He made Jesus to be a light to the whole world. We find this in both the New Testament and the Old.[17] In the end, God will call people of all nations His own, even those who were once Israel's enemies.[18]

Stripes

Next, there is a biblical case to be made that the punishments for sin will not be equal for every sinner. Jesus told the Pharisees that they would receive the greater damnation because of their hypocrisy. They were supposed to be the spiritual leaders, and they acted holy by giving long prayers, but they would then blatantly disregard God's Law by taking the houses of widows.

> *Woe unto you, scribes and Pharisees,*
> *hypocrites! for ye devour widows' houses,*
> *and for a pretence make long prayer:*
> *therefore ye shall receive the greater*
> *damnation.*
>
> Matthew 23:14

James even warns about becoming a leader of others, because those who lead will be judged more harshly than those who follow them. Leaders are held to a higher standard, because people look to them for guidance.

*My brethren, be not many masters,
knowing that we shall receive the greater
condemnation.*

James 3:1

Jesus tells us that those who have greater knowledge will be punished more harshly than those who know less:

*And that servant, which knew his lord's
will, and prepared not himself, neither
did according to his will, shall be beaten
with many stripes. But he that knew not,
and did commit things worthy of stripes,
shall be beaten with few stripes. For unto
whomsoever much is given, of him shall be
much required: and to whom men have
committed much, of him they will ask
the more.*

Luke 12:47-48

We are therefore responsible for the knowledge we've been given, and we are less responsible for the knowledge we're not given. At the same time, wisdom dictates that we seek God out ourselves. This includes all people everywhere — because God honors those who seek Him, wherever they are.

Diligence Rewarded

Hebrews 11:6 tells us that God rewards those who diligently hunt for Him. Whether we live among the pagan cultures of Sumatra or among the pagan cultures of Seattle, we should desire to know who God is and what His will is for our lives. Jesus told us clearly in Matthew 7:8, "*For every one that asketh receiveth; and he that seeketh findeth; and to him that knocketh it shall be opened.*" God will not turn away or ignore those who long to find Him.

That doesn't mean we will hear from God immediately. We have all spent weeks and months and sometimes years searching for His guidance, His wisdom, His touch. There are times He requires us to be patient and wait on Him. Hebrews tells us God rewards those who *diligently* seek Him. However, there are many verses in the Bible that offer this same theme: those who earnestly look for God will find Him:

> *The LORD is good unto them that wait for him, to the soul that seeketh him.*
>
> Lamentations 3:25

> *And ye shall seek me, and find me, when ye shall search for me with all your heart.*
>
> Jeremiah 29:13

> *If ye then, being evil, know how to give good gifts unto your children: how much more shall your heavenly Father give the Holy Spirit to them that ask him?*
>
> Luke 11:13

> *...for he who comes to God must believe that He is, and that He is a rewarder of those who diligently seek Him.*
>
> Hebrews 11:6

> *Wait on the LORD: be of good courage, and he shall strengthen thine heart: wait, I say, on the LORD.*
>
> Psalm 27:14

There is a famous story that has circulated for years about a young man named Chaluba from a family of idol makers.[19] Chaluba had been carving little wooden gods since he was a child. One day as Chaluba carved an idol from wood, he realized that he had the power to either carve or destroy the god he had made with his own hands. He looked at his hands, knowing that they too had been made by Somebody. He decided then to find the God who had made his hands. He stopped carving idols and refused to worship the village gods, because he didn't want to worship gods he could destroy. He only wanted to worship the God who had made his hands.

Chaluba spent years on his hunt for this God, traveling and eventually learning to read. People had heard of the God who made the jungle and everything in it, but they could not tell Chaluba much about Him. He learned there was book he could read, however, that would tell him about this God. Eventually, missionaries brought Bibles, and he was able to read about the God who created the heavens and the earth, who gave His Son to die for us.

Chaluba didn't find God the very day he went looking for Him. It took many years for Chaluba to track down somebody who could tell him about the God who made his hands. However, God rewarded Chaluba's years of diligent searching, and Chaluba came to know Jesus as his Savior. Chaluba was raised in the jungle among idol makers, far from any Christian church, yet God was faithful to that young man. And even though Chaluba was raised in the remote jungle, his story has gone into all the world.

The Creation

We know that God will judge us based on the knowledge that has been given us. The people in the Old Testament didn't know about Jesus, but they trusted in the words that Moses and the prophets gave them from God. They trusted in the knowledge God had provided for them.

However, everybody in the world should be able to recognize the character and nature of God — if only through the things He has made. Paul makes this argument, saying:

> *For the invisible things of him from the creation of the world are clearly seen, being understood by the things that are made, even his eternal power and Godhead; so that they are without excuse:*
>
> Romans 1:20

We can all know who God is by what He has made. There is no excuse, because His brilliance can be found all around us. Before we understood about DNA or could look at the miniature cities of activity inside each cell, we could still see order and beauty and constancy in the world. The sun always rises, every morning. We can depend on gravity and other physical forces. Flowers grow, even in the desert and on rocky cliff faces. Millions of tons of fruit and nuts and other natural edibles fall to the ground without being eaten every year, and there are stars so far out in the universe we're only now seeing their light. The world that God created is filled with beauty, abundance, variety and mercy. We can know God's character by the world He has made — and that's even after the world has been corrupted by sin!

Written on our Hearts

We also all know right and wrong, because it's been written on our hearts. We can try to justify our evil deeds, but in all cultures around the world, it's understood that adultery, murder, deception and cruelty are wrong. In Genesis 20, before the Law was given, we find that Abraham has allowed Abimelech the king of Gerar, in Canaan, to take Sarah. God threatens Abimelech in a dream, because he has taken another man's wife. Abimelech defends himself, saying, "I didn't know! He told me she was his sister!" God tells him, "I know. That's why I didn't let you touch her."

Abimelech didn't argue with God about whether it was okay for him to take another man's wife. This particular Canaanite king knew it was wrong to do so, and he was a righteous man who wouldn't do such a thing. God put the fear into Abimelech over the matter, but He also protected Abimelech from committing a grave sin in ignorance.

Also note that God didn't have Abraham take over Canaan during Abimelech's time. It took several hundred years for corruption to completely overtake Canaan. Four hundred years after Abraham's great grandchildren moved into Egypt, God-fearing leaders like Abimelech were all gone.

Pay attention to what Paul tells us in Romans 2:

For as many as have sinned without law shall also perish without law: and as many as have sinned in the law shall be judged by the law; (For not the hearers of the law are just before God, but the doers of the law shall be justified.

For when the Gentiles, which have not the law, do by nature the things contained in the law, these, having not the law, are a law unto themselves: Which shew the work of the law written in their hearts, their conscience also bearing witness, and their thoughts the mean while accusing or else excusing one another;) In the day when God shall judge the secrets of men by Jesus Christ according to my gospel.

Romans 2:121-16

We are not justified by our works. All have sinned and fallen short of the glory of God.[20] Paul starts to explain this in the next chapter of Romans. However, those who love righteousness are all capable of recognizing their own failure to obtain true righteousness. All are capable of recognizing there is a God who created the world, and of seeking God's forgiveness for the times they have erred.

Of course, few of us would realize anything if somebody had not come along and told us the truth. We human beings tend to be dense. It's important for us to get out there and let the world know that God is alive and well and is still doing things in human lives. We need to let them know that Jesus is the Savior who gave His life for our sins. We need to follow the leading of the Holy Spirit, who loves the people in our lives. We don't want anybody to die without Christ simply because they didn't know.

Ultimately, we trust that God is wise, and that He sees into the heart of every human on the earth. The Lord does not judge by outward appearances, but by the heart. He will judge righteously.

> *Henceforth there is laid up for me a crown of righteousness, which the Lord, the righteous judge, shall give me at that day: and not to me only, but unto all them also that love his appearing.*
>
> 2 Timothy 4:8

Chapter 8
The God Outside of Time

Imagine you're sitting on a curb watching a parade. Around the corner come the marching band, the Boy Scouts, and the fire trucks all in order. As they march on by you, you experience the parade as a sequence of events. You can watch each group turn the corner and walk down the street in front of you and then turn another corner up ahead.

It *is* possible to see all the groups at once, though. It just requires heading to a higher plane of existence. A helicopter hovering over the parade or the people at the top of a Ferris wheel will be able to see the entire sequence of the parade. With one look around, they can see the staging area where the marching units are forming up all the way to the end of the road where the groups disband. This is a clumsy analogy, but it helps us understand how having access to another dimension offers a range of improved capabilities.

We forget sometimes, I think, that God doesn't look at us moment-to-moment. He looks at us from outside the time domain altogether. He sees who we are in eternity. He sees all of human history as we might see a comic strip. He can see the end from the beginning in one glance. He's able to reach into our lives in the moment, and He does so because time matters to *us*. However, He's the beginning and the end of all things, and He doesn't look at things the way that human beings do.[21]

> *Remember the former things of old: for I am God, and there is none else; I am God, and there is none like me, Declaring the end from the beginning, and from ancient times the things that are not yet done, saying, My counsel shall stand, and I will do all my pleasure:*
>
> Isaiah 46:9-10

Outside Time

All of us made timelines in school. So, when we encounter the concept of eternity, we tend to imagine it as a line. It starts at infinity on the left and goes to infinity on the right. We think of "eternity" as lots and lots of time — an unlimited amount of time. We sing "Amazing Grace" declaring, "When we've been there 10,000 years bright shining as the sun, we've no less days to sing God's grace than when we'd first begun." That makes colorful poetry, but it's not quite correct.

As we consider the question of the afterlife, we need to realize that time is a physical quality. It's the fourth dimension, and eternity is outside of that time dimension altogether.

I want to take some brief paragraphs exploring this peculiar thing we call Time. People often have questions like, "What is the spirit realm? Where is it? Isn't it just the creation of somebody's active imagination?" Understanding the nature of time and space is important in knowing how to answer these sorts of questions, even if just for ourselves.

There is a cesium clock at the National Institute of Standards and Technology in Boulder, Colorado and another at the National Physics Laboratory (NPL) in Teddington, England (19 miles across London from the old Royal Observatory in Greenwich). As technology has improved, the engineers have made these devices increasingly accurate. In 1955, the world's first atomic clock at the British NPL was accurate to one second in 300 years. In comparison, the NIST-F2 clock launched in Boulder in 2014 was reported not to lose or gain a second in about 300 million years.[22]

We might ask, "Who cares?" It turns out that the accuracy of time measurement is very important. It determines the precision of our navigation systems. The timing of these devices ensures the accuracy of global positioning satellite systems, and those nanoseconds are significant when our phone tells us, "Make a right in 50 feet."

This measurement of time is based on the natural resonance of the cesium atom. That's what gives these clocks their incredible precision. Yet, we observe something very interesting. These two clocks, the one in Teddington and the one in Boulder, are extremely accurate, and yet, the one in Boulder ticks five millionths of a second every year faster than its twin in England. The difference is predictable and measurable, and it begs us to ask which clock is the correct one. The fact is, they are both correct.

The clocks in Boulder and Teddington are a shade off from each other, because Boulder is at an elevation of 5,430 ft. (1,655 m), and Teddington is less than 100 ft. (30 m) above sea level. It turns out that time itself is different at sea level than it is at a mile in elevation, because time changes with gravity. If I had an atomic clock and I raised it one meter, it would speed up by one part in 10^{16}. That's not enough to change our schedules, but it's profoundly significant in understanding the nature of time. Even the difference in elevation is affected by the gravity involved. Which brings us to Einstein's general theory of relativity.

Physics books often give the example of hypothetical twin astronauts. One astronaut remains on Earth, but his twin flies off in a spacecraft to the nearest star, Alpha Centauri, at half the speed of light. This star is about 4½ light years away, which means that the trip there should take the astronaut twin nine years. The trip back is another nine years, and so the astronaut twin should be gone a total of 18 years from our perspective on Earth. It turns out, however, that the experience of the star-traveling twin is a bit different. According to the clock he keeps on the spacecraft, the entire trip has taken him just 15 years and seven months. I won't go through the

Lorentz transformations to explain the math, but time has dilated for the twin traveling at half the speed of light. Time has stretched, and so it runs slower when compared to time passing on Earth. The second twin will return to Earth two years and five months younger than his brother.

Let's say we could send the astronaut twin to Alpha Centauri at 99.99% the speed of light. While the trip would take a full nine years from our perspective on earth, the trip would take just 33 days from the space traveling twin's reference frame because of relativity.

Time is a physical dimension. Space and time can both stretch and bend, but they are as connected as the width, length, and height of a box. Time stretches and slows as one travels closer to the speed of light, because spatial dimensions like length and width get shorter. If a child steps on ball, its sides push out. If two children pull on opposite sides of a shirt, the shirt lengthens, but it narrows in the middle to compensate.

In his theory of special relativity in 1905, Einstein told us that mass, velocity and time are relative to the observer, and light speed is the same for all observers, no matter how fast they're going. Then, in his general theory of relativity in 1915, Einstein described a new theory of gravity, in which gravity is the warping of space-time.

This is all important, because Einstein realized that we don't just live in only three dimensions. However, Einstein didn't go far enough.

The German mathematician Theodor Kaluza noticed that by adding a fifth dimension to Einstein's field equations, he was able to naturally produce Maxwell's equations on electromagnetism. Kaluza suspected that there was an additional dimension *into which* space was bending. If space can bend and warp, it has to be bending and warping into another dimension. 1926 Oskar Kline added a quantum flavor to Kaluza's ideas, and the Kaluza-Kline theory described electromagnetism as gravity curled up in the fifth dimension.

It continued from there. In 1953, Wolfgang Pauli played around with extending Kaluza and Klein's five dimensions to six. Further research has revealed that our universe probably exists in about 10 dimensions. At least five possible string theories became popular during the 1980s. In 1995, Witten suggested that the five string theories were actually just different faces of a single theory which he called M-theory (for Magic / Mystery / Matrix Theory). M-Theory predicts at least 10 dimensions (3+1+6), or 11 if we count supergravity.[23]

Quantum Entanglement

There is more evidence for additional dimensions than just skilled mathematical gymnastics. Even during Einstein's time, physicists started to see that entangled particles — paired up photons or electrons — seemed to be instantly communicating with each other. That is, each particle seemed to know what was happening to the other particle, and they knew it faster than the speed of light. Einstein didn't like this. He called it "spooky action at a distance." With two other physicists, he made the case that the particles were not actually communicating instantly, they just *looked* like they were. In his famous "EPR" paper, Einstein said that quantum mechanics was just an incomplete study, and there were "hidden variables" — a sort of particle DNA programming — that determined how the paired particles would behave in advance.[24] It turns out Einstein was wrong about this.

John Stewart Bell decided to figure out whether or not the particles had hidden variables. He didn't have the technology to directly observe the particles making their decisions, but he came up with an experiment that could indirectly give him the answer he needed based on probabilities.[25] It turns out that the particles were indeed instantly communicating — faster than the speed of light.

What does that mean to us? To make a clumsy analogy, it's as though the particles are physically connected to each other in another dimension, like the threads of a rug. We see only the particles as points on the end of the rug tassels, but they are connected where the tassels meet to form the rug. They only appear to be separated and magically communicating by "spooky action at a distance" because we only see the tips. We can't see where they're connected in an additional dimension.

In 1982, Alain Aspect, Jean Dalibard, and Gérard Roger at the Institute of Theoretical and Applied Optics in Paris, conducted a landmark experiment — the so-called two-particle experiment — which directly demonstrated that Bell was right.[26] In recent years with better technology, scientists have been able to catch the particles in the act of instantaneous communication, and this is the basis for the new science of quantum computing.

In a BBC interview, Bell said, "It is as if there is some kind of conspiracy, that something is going on behind the scenes which is not allowed to appear on the scenes. And I agree that's extremely uncomfortable."[27]

Angels

The Bible has *many* indications that we live in more dimensions than we can directly experience. When angels step into the visible world, they always have physical bodies. They led Lot and his family by the hand in Genesis 19. In Genesis 18:8 and 19:1-3, we read that they are able to eat. The Angel of the Lord is responsible for killing the 185,000 Assyrians sent against Jerusalem in 2 Kings 19:35. Yet, angels are able to slip out of our physical world just as easily as they appear. The warrior angel who appears in Daniel 10 describes warfare beyond the sight of our physical eyes. This indicates that the universe has a greater dimensionality than we are generally privy to.

The Bible never says point blank, "There are more dimensions than you humans can experience right now." It doesn't say it directly, but there are a multitude of clues.

Stretching the Heavens

We find the idea that God stretches out the heavens all throughout the Bible. When we talk about the "fabric" of space-time, we shouldn't look at it as just a metaphor. Consider the following verses:

> *Which alone spreadeth out the heavens, and treadeth upon the waves of the sea.*
>
> Job 9:8

> *Bless the LORD, O my soul. O LORD my God, thou art very great; thou art clothed with honour and majesty. Who coverest thyself with light as with a garment: who stretchest out the heavens like a curtain:*
>
> Psalm 104:1-2

> *It is he that sitteth upon the circle of the earth, and the inhabitants thereof are as grasshoppers; that stretcheth out the heavens as a curtain, and spreadeth them out as a tent to dwell in:*
>
> Isaiah 40:22

> *He hath made the earth by his power, he hath established the world by his wisdom,*

and hath stretched out the heavens by his discretion.

Jeremiah 10:12

The burden of the word of the LORD for Israel, saith the LORD, which stretcheth forth the heavens, and layeth the foundation of the earth, and formeth the spirit of man within him.

Zechariah 12:1

We tend to imagine a nothingness out there between the planets and stars, and we speak of the empty vacuum of space. However, Einstein's theory of general relativity describes gravity as the bending of space-time. The 20th century taught us that space-time is a fabric, but for thousands of years the Bible has already said as much. We find space can be:

Torn	Isaiah 64:1
Worn out like a garment	Psalm 102:25-26
Shaken	Isaiah 13:13; Haggai 2:6; Hebrews 12:26
Burnt up	2 Peter 3:12
Rolled up	Isaiah 34:4; Revelation 6:14

Today we know that space has physical properties. "Empty" space contains more energy than we can imagine. There is energy buzzing in each cubic centimeter of space, even when every bit of heat is removed and the system has been reduced to a temperature of 0 Kelvin. This energy that remains at absolute zero is called the "zero-point energy" (ZPE) and Barry Setterfield uses the following explanation to help us understand its immensity:

> A bright light bulb radiates at 150 watts. By contrast, our sun radiates at 3.8×10^{26} watts. In our galaxy there are 100 billion stars. If they all radiate at about the same intensity as our sun, then the amount of energy expended by our entire galaxy of stars shining for 10 billion years is roughly the energy locked up in one cubic centimeter of space. The physical vacuum is not just an empty nothingness.[28]

That's beyond comprehension.

We cannot feel the ZPE because its power is balanced evenly all around us. It's the same case with air pressure. If the 14.7 psi of air pressure around us pushed straight down on us, it would crush us. However, because air pressure is pushing in every direction, it all balances out. The same goes for the ZPE. It is perfectly balanced all around us, keeping the energy of 100 billion stars shining for 10 billion years in check. I wonder how many physicists consider the immensity of the ZPE and think about its implications regarding the nature of reality.

The Bible tells us that space is like a fabric that can be torn and shaken and worn out. Isaiah and Revelation also tell us that space can be rolled up. If it can be rolled up, there must be some additional dimension into which it can be rolled, just like Kaluza thought! If I have a two-dimensional piece of paper, I cannot roll it up into a tube unless I have a third dimension to roll into. If the four dimensions of space-time can be rolled up, then there must be an additional dimension into which it can be bent. These hints are already in the Scripture.

Charlie Brown and Lucy think of their world in terms of two dimensions, because that's what they are used to. They cannot see us watching them from our vantage point in three dimensions. We can reach down and touch Charlie Brown or Lucy in different frames at the same time if we want, even if they are on the comic pages of completely different Sunday morning newspapers. It's only when our finger enters their 2D domain that they can see us — and even then, they can only see our finger as a circle. They can't see the whole thing. They can't see the whole us.

We think of eternity in terms of three dimensions because that's what we're used to. However, Heaven and Hell exist outside our four-dimensional space-time.

When we are with God in Heaven, there will be no time. Time will no longer exist. It's also important to understand, because Heaven and Hell are real places. They exist in a dimensionality greater than the four we directly experience. The spiritual realm is not an imaginary, ethereal place. It is a reality beyond our simple ability to imagine.

The Word of God

God is not somebody who has a lot of time. Isaiah 57:15 tells us that He inhabits eternity. We recognize that when the Holy Spirit breathed the words of the Bible, He did so from beyond the walls of our space-time dwelling.

Many people hear about Heaven and Hell and Jesus' death on the cross, but they don't know if any of it is true. They don't know whether the Bible is God's Word or not. This is another reason why it's important for us to understand that God is eternal. It is *because* God exists outside of time that He is able to authenticate His message to us. We can know that the Bible really is the Word of God, because throughout human history, God has told us things in advance. He made this clear through Isaiah:

> *Remember the former things of old: for I am God, and there is none else; I am God, and there is none like me, Declaring the end from the beginning, and from ancient times the things that are not yet done, saying, My counsel shall stand, and I will do all my pleasure:*

> Isaiah 46:9-10

God authenticates his message by writing history before it happens. He demonstrates that the origin of His Word is from outside the fourth dimension. I recommend several of our studies that look at this more in-depth, because the Bible's precision fascinates me — and I suspect it will fascinate you too.[29]

The scholars of the 19th century found it in vogue to discount the books of the Old Testament as relatively young works written centuries or millennia after the events they purported to describe. They told us that Moses did not write the first five books of the Bible, because writing did not even exist in his time. They said that Isaiah did not write Isaiah and Daniel did not write Daniel. Without much evidence but a great deal of skepticism, they denied not only the inspiration of the Scriptures, but even their historical accuracy.

Modern scholarship has proved much friendlier to the books of the Bible. Archeology has demonstrated the historical trustworthiness of the Bible's books. Modern orthography and language analysis have demonstrated the great age of books like Daniel and Isaiah, and it turns out that writing did exist during the time of Moses after all.[30]

Our ministry is based on two primary discoveries. The book we glibly call the Bible is made up of 66 books penned by more than 40 different writers over virtually 2000 years, and yet it's an integrated message system. The Bible doesn't simply have a consistent theme. It turns out that every number, every place name, every detail is there by skillful engineering.

The second discovery derives from the first. If the 66 books of the Bible are an integrated message — even though they were written by dozens of different people, in different locations and time periods; then it must be a message from outside our time dimension. Once you discover these things for yourself, they open up a much greater perspective on what we call The Word of God.

In a letter to the family of a friend that had died, Albert Einstein once wrote, "Now he has departed from this strange world a little ahead of me. That means nothing. People like us, who believe in physics, know that the distinction between past, present, and future is only a stubbornly persistent illusion." His purpose was to comfort the family after their loss. However, it's true. When we recognize there are dimensions beyond the ones we can see directly, we can understand the very concept of time is unique to our particular situation, our particular predicament in reality.

Chapter 9
At the Cross

What exactly happened at the cross? We know that Jesus died, that He paid for our sins. His blood covers us so that when the Father looks at us, He doesn't see our sin, He sees Christ's sacrifice. The writer of Hebrews goes into this subject in depth, because the sacrificial system of the Old Testament was never meant to cleanse sin of itself. It was merely meant to help us understand sacrificial atonement. It was meant to be a place holder in the minds of the people until Christ came as the ultimate sacrifice.

A variety of other things took place when Jesus died, however, and I want to look at those. Many conservative Bible scholars believe that between the time that Jesus died on the cross and rose again that Sunday morning, He emptied Abraham's Bosom. I believe there is justification for the argument that He took those faithful that were accumulated in Abraham's bosom to Himself. Remember what He said to the thief on the cross, "Verily I say unto thee, Today shalt thou be with me in paradise."[31] The thief was going to be with Him in paradise that same day.

In I Peter 3, Peter writes:

For Christ also hath once suffered for sins, the just for the unjust, that he might bring us to God, being put to death in the flesh, but quickened by the Spirit: By which also he went and preached unto the spirits in prison; Which sometime were disobedient, when once the longsuffering of God waited in the days of Noah, while the ark was a preparing, wherein few, that is, eight souls were saved by water.

1 Peter 3:18-20

We have to be careful about our understanding of the word "preached" here. We tend to think of preaching as an effort to change somebody's mind. That's not the meaning here. Here it just means "to declare." Jesus entered Hell to declare His victory on the cross and His victory over death. This victory was prophesied long in advance. Jesus came to free those souls from prison.

When Jesus opened His ministry in Nazareth in Luke 4, He opened the scroll of Isaiah to the verses we now call Isaiah 61:1-2a:

The Spirit of the Lord GOD is upon me; because the LORD hath anointed me to preach good tidings unto the meek; he hath sent me to bind up the brokenhearted, to proclaim liberty to the captives, and the opening of the prison to them that are bound; To proclaim the acceptable year of the LORD...

Isaiah 61:1-2a

That's where the Lord stops. I like to say that Jesus stopped at a comma, because He really just ends in the middle of the sentence. He doesn't continue to read the next phrase in the verse, "*and the day of vengeance of our God...*" His mandate during His ministry was just to that comma. He came to proclaim liberty to the captives and to free those who are bound. It's at the Second Coming that He'll enact the day of vengeance. That's still in the future, and in the meanwhile we still have a chance to run to Him.

As we consider these things, I want to point out an interesting passage in Matthew 27:

Jesus, when he had cried again with a loud voice, yielded up the ghost. And, behold, the veil of the temple was rent in twain from the top to the bottom; and the earth did quake, and the rocks rent; And the graves were opened; and many bodies of the saints which slept arose, And came out of the graves after his resurrection, and went into the holy city, and appeared unto many. Now when the centurion, and they that were with him, watching Jesus, saw the earthquake, and those things that were done, they feared greatly, saying, Truly this was the Son of God.

Matthew 27:50-54

This is an odd set of descriptions, and Matthew is the only one to mention them. We have no other references to these events, we can only speculate about what they signify.

We know that when Jesus arose on Sunday morning, He fulfilled the Feast of Firstfruits, as foreordained on the Sunday after the Passover.[32] He became the first One risen from the dead. Paul makes this clear to us, in case we missed it.

> *For as in Adam all die, even so in Christ all shall be made alive. But each one in his own order: Christ the firstfruits, afterward those who are Christ's at His coming.*
> 1 Corinthians 15:22-23

The word firstfruits is plural. It may be that some of those who broke out of their graves were in Abraham's bosom until then, and they became part of Christ's firstfruits there on that Resurrection Sunday. Perhaps.

Chapter 10
Day of Judgment

When Jesus came the first time, it was to set the captives free. He is still setting people free to this day — free from sin and death, free from addiction and broken hearts, disease and all manner of other chains and prisons. Jesus has spent 2000 years rescuing lost humans. However, there will be a day when it's all over. The day will come when we all have to stand before Him to be evaluated on the content of our lives. We all will face a judgment day.

Let's talk a little bit about the justice of God.

God the Father has given all authority and power to Jesus Christ.[33] This is tremendously comforting, because we know that Jesus will judge based on what is true. God the Father loves us and sent His Son to die for us, and Jesus died willingly in our place. This is good news. The bad news is that too many people have failed to place themselves under His mercy and will die in their sins.

All religions do not lead to salvation. They don't all lead to Heaven. However, all religions do lead to God and His judgment seat. Buddha and Confucius and Mohammed will be in our same position as created beings. They will be among those facing an appraisal of their lives, and Jesus Christ will be the lawyer and judge.

The Bible is very clear about this fact. Every person is going to be resurrected and judged individually. Every hour of life, all our words spoken in secret, every hidden thought and every motive will be made public. Our deeds and misdeeds will be tried in the perfect court, where there are no misinterpretations and no getting off on technicalities. All blame will be accurately proportioned. There'll be no unsolved crimes and no hidden bribes.

When it comes to the Judgment, we find a constant theme of making the invisible visible. Those things that were done in secret will be made known — whether they were good or whether they were evil:

> *But thou, when thou prayest, enter into thy closet, and when thou hast shut thy door, pray to thy Father which is in secret; and thy Father which seeth in secret shall reward thee openly.*
>
> Matthew 6:6
>
> *For there is nothing covered, that shall not be revealed; neither hid, that shall not be known. Therefore whatsoever ye have spoken in darkness shall be heard in the light; and that which ye have spoken in the*

ear in closets shall be proclaimed upon the housetops.

Luke 12:2-3

Also I say unto you, Whosoever shall confess me before men, him shall the Son of man also confess before the angels of God: But he that denieth me before men shall be denied before the angels of God.

Luke 12:8-9

Two Judgements

At the same time, it's important to realize that there are two judgment seats: the Great White Throne, and the Bema Seat. Those who have died in their sins will be judged at the Great White Throne (Rev. 20:11-12) according to their sins, and their misdeeds will be manifest to all the universe. Before that, those who belong to Christ will be rewarded at the Bema Seat of Christ (1 Cor. 5:9-12, Rom. 14:10) for pleasing God by doing His will.

Remember, those who have died in Christ have had all their sins covered. Those sins are blotted out.[34] Psalms 103:12 tells us, "As far as the east is from the west, so far hath he removed our transgressions from us." Those who are in Christ Jesus will not be judged based on their sins, because their sins are gone. Micah 7:19 tells us that God will cast those sins "into the depths of the sea." It's the sea of forgetfulness. Therefore, those who are saved will simply be judged on the works they did in God's service.

The Great White Throne

In Revelation 10, John describes the Great White Throne. All people, one-time important rulers and slaves alike, are pulled from Sheol and from the earth to be judged and consigned to their eternal state. This is the final exam. Jesus tells us that every idle word that people have spoken will be examined. Boy, that's scary.

But I say unto you, That every idle word that men shall speak, they shall give account thereof in the day of judgment.
Matthew 12:36

The wrath of God will be revealed against all ungodliness. Jesus had to die, because the wages of sin is death.[35] God does not wink at sin. He deals with it.

For the wrath of God is revealed from heaven against all ungodliness and unrighteousness of men, who hold the truth in unrighteousness; Because that which may be known of God is manifest in them; for God hath shewed it unto them… Because that, when they knew God, they glorified him not as God, neither were thankful; but became vain in their imaginations, and their foolish heart was

> *darkened. Professing themselves to be wise, they became fools…*
>
> Romans 1:18-19; 21-22

This is all coming home to roost at the final Judgment. There will be no exceptions. Everybody will be there, and everybody will be held accountable according to the knowledge they were given. Here is the description of that Judgment Day in Revelation 20:

> *And I saw a great white throne, and him that sat on it, from whose face the earth and the heaven fled away; and there was found no place for them. And I saw the dead, small and great, stand before God; and the books were opened: and another book was opened, which is the book of life: and the dead were judged out of those things which were written in the books, according to their works. And the sea gave up the dead which were in it; and death and hell delivered up the dead which were in them: and they were judged every man according to their works. And death and hell were cast into the lake of fire. This is the second death. And whosoever was not found written in the book of life was cast into the lake of fire.*
>
> Revelation 20:12-15

This is a serious business.

When he wrote his great work of literature, *Divine Comedy,* Dante Alighieri had some ideas that aren't actually biblical. However, he did get some things correct. In *Inferno,* the first part of the *Divine Comedy,* Dante gets to take a tour through Hell as a living being on a divine mission. As he enters, there is a sign over the door that says, "*Lasciate ogne speranza, voi ch'intrate*" commonly translated "Abandon all hope who enter here." While Dante's ideas of Hell are the work of a great imagination, that is an accurate concept.

We have no ability to imagine what it's like to be without hope. I was once able to visit the world's largest maximum-security prison. There were men there who had sat on death row for more than a decade. Even there, a smidgen of hope still existed. Even in that hopeless position, the men seemed to cling to the thread of a chance that the governor might sign their pardon before the day of their termination. The old saying, "Where there's life, there's hope" rings true. However, after death and the Judgment, there's no more hope. You and I can't imagine the utter sense of despair that is entailed in an eternity with no more chances.

Right now, on earth, we have difficult times. We have times when we are at the bottom of ourselves and see no way out. We all come to those places in life. However, even in those times the sun still shines overhead. There's rain to water the earth. We know that somewhere on the planet, we can find somebody willing to give us a shred of kindness. God is still here, all around us, ready to show us mercy. We can't imagine being disconnected from the source of all life for eternity. We can't imagine complete separation from the movement of the Holy Spirit that fills us and gives us joy even in the darkness. We can't imagine being permanently exiled from Him.

We know that the second death is about retributive justice. It's the punishment for disobedience and rejection of God's provision. God has to punish wickedness. He has to vindicate His holiness. He is the King of the Universe whose very nature is righteousness and truth, and justice must either be performed or paid for. God has a moral order that must be upheld. This is no joke. As much as God loves us, He loves His Son more, and yet He was willing to give Him to save us. If we refuse that offering made in our place, then God cannot compromise. He has to allow those who die in their sins to accept their own punishment. He is holy, and since God is holy, He must reassert the moral order against all that is evil.

Eternal Punishment

Even though we understand these things, it is difficult for us to get our minds around the idea of punishment that lasts for eternity. It seems that the punishment doesn't fit the crimes. People have sinned against God and committed violations against His righteousness. We understand that, but we cannot grasp that the punishment for those crimes will last forever. We all have difficulty with this.

It therefore begs a different question: do we really understand God's attitude towards sin? I don't think so. Remember, adultery was a capital crime in Israel. We wouldn't even think of stoning somebody in our culture today. We can't handle that, and if we could we'd probably cut the population of adults in half tomorrow. The use of séances or attempts to speak to the dead was a capital crime, as was the use of horoscopes! We treat horoscopes as silly newspaper entertainment. In ancient Israel, to cast a horoscope made the offender subject to punishment by stoning.

God doesn't mess around when it comes to sin. He takes these things seriously. Our sensitivities to sin are calloused. I believe in life, liberty and the pursuit of happiness, but in our culture, we have placed man's desires above God's Word. We fail to understand two things. On one hand, we don't understand the magnitude of evil involved in our sins. On the other hand — we have no appreciation for the majesty of God.

Part of the seriousness of sin isn't just the destruction it causes. It's serious because it is direct rebellion against the holiness of the infinite God. This is an immensely important subject. God is love, and God loves the fallen human race. However, the God who is deserving of all worship and honor cannot issue arbitrary amnesty for humanitarians or pantheists who persist in worshiping and serving themselves more than the Creator Himself.

Those who are lost will not simply have to answer for their sins. They will have to answer for having disregarded God's revealed will. Whether they have heard the Word of God, or whether they simply have the witness of the creation itself, they will be responsible for the revelation they've been given.

> *For we must all appear before the judgment seat of Christ; that every one may receive the things done in his body, according to that he hath done, whether it be good or bad.*
>
> 2 Corinthians 5:10

The Bema Seat

In the ancient Olympics, a judge would sit on the finish line in what was known as the Bema Seat. This position gave him a clear view of who crossed the line first, second, third and so on, so he could then hand out the deserved awards.

Paul treats our efforts for Christ in terms of a race we are trying to win. He says:

> *And this I do for the gospel's sake, that I might be partaker thereof with you. Know ye not that they which run in a race run all, but one receiveth the prize? So run, that ye may obtain. And every man that striveth for the mastery is*

temperate in all things. Now they do it to obtain a corruptible crown; but we an incorruptible.

1 Corinthians 9:23-25

Jesus described the judgment of His servants on several occasions, using parables as was His custom.

In the famous parable of the talents in Matthew 25:14-30, the Lord describes a master who has gone to a far country and has left his servants with various amounts of money to invest while he's gone. When he returns, he calls his servants to him and has them give an account of themselves. One faithful servant has doubled the five talents he was given, and he is able to show ten talents to the master. Another faithful servant has doubled the two talents he was given, and he is able to present four talents to the master. The master is pleased with both of these servants who made the most of what they were given. He tells each of them, "Well done, good and faithful servant; thou hast been faithful over a few things, I will make thee ruler over many things: enter thou into the joy of thy lord."

It's the final servant who gets into trouble. He has buried his one talent and refused to work with it because he figured the master would just take the fruit of his labor. He clearly has no love for the master, no good expectations of the master, no desire to serve him well. While the man richly rewarded the first two servants, this lazy servant is cast into outer darkness.

We find another rendition of this parable in Luke 19:12-27.

This is not about earning salvation. The faithless servant didn't simply fail to perform. He demonstrated the true state of his heart. That's what our works always are — they are a demonstration of what's in our hearts. Is our heart filled with the love of God and a love for God, or is our heart filled with bitter, stony selfishness?

In 1 Corinthians 3, Paul gives us a good set of visuals regarding the Bema Seat judgment. He treats our works as though they are material items. The foundation of our salvation is faith in Christ, and we can all get into Heaven with that foundation alone. However, we are also laborers *"together with God"* in constructing a single, magnificent building on the foundation of Jesus Christ. That building is made of those who are saved — we are the treasures in its walls. All the work we do to grow the kingdom adds more building materials to the whole structure. For the past 2000 years, this building has been growing, and more and more people are added to the kingdom as we serve God in loving those around us and leading them to Christ.

Now, some of our building materials might be made of useless junk, things we did out of selfishness or self-promotion. Some of our building materials might be made of beautiful gems, things that we did out of love and devotion and faithful obedience. Here is exactly what Paul says:

> *For we are labourers together with God: ye are God's husbandry, ye are God's building. According to the grace of God which is given unto me, as a wise masterbuilder, I have laid the foundation, and another buildeth thereon. But let every man take heed how he buildeth thereupon. For other foundation can no man lay than that is laid, which is Jesus Christ.*
>
> 1 Corinthians 3:9-11

Remember, we're not trying to earn our salvation here. Jesus is the foundation for everything — for our salvation, for our hope, for our labor. When we do work in the Lord, we are adding to the work that the apostles did at the very beginning.

> *Now if any man build upon this foundation gold, silver, precious stones, wood, hay, stubble; Every man's work shall be made manifest: for the day shall declare it, because it shall be revealed by fire; and the fire shall try every man's work of what sort it is. If any man's work abide which he hath built thereupon, he shall receive a reward. If any man's work shall be burned, he shall suffer loss: but he himself shall be*

saved; yet so as by fire. Know ye not that ye are the temple of God, and that the Spirit of God dwelleth in you?

1 Corinthians 3:12-16

There it is. It will be clear on that day what kind of work we've done. There will most likely be some wood, hay and stubble in all of our building materials. However, the goal of our lives is to serve God well — to represent Him well, to obey the leading of the Holy Spirit and to lay down our lives by setting aside our pride and selfish ambitions. We want to add gold and rubies and sapphires to the building. We want our lives to be a labor of gratitude for the Savior who loved us and gave His life for us. If we follow Him, He will lead us in bringing people into His kingdom, because He loves them. *Because we love Him*, we don't want Him to lose any of His lambs.

On that day, when God sets fire to the whole thing, all that is beautiful and worthy will be left. The wood, hay and stubble will burn up. Whether our works burn up or not, we are saved, but I'm certain in that day, we will be glad to see gemstones shining bright in our portion of the vast building.

Wherefore seeing we also are compassed about with so great a cloud of witnesses, let us lay aside every weight, and the sin which doth so easily beset us, and let us run with patience the race that is set before us...

Hebrew 12:1

Chapter 11
What We Shall Be

Life eternal. That sounds good. We might forget that the life Christ offers isn't just everlasting, it's everlasting in a new, strong, remarkable body.

Jesus demonstrated some interesting abilities after He rose from the dead. He still appeared in his human, physical, three-dimensional form to the disciples, because that's what they were able to see. However, the things He did after He rose clearly show that He had obtained extra-dimensional abilities. When we can join Jesus where He is, we'll be able to see Him as He really is (1 John 3:2), and that will be an exciting day.

Even before we go to Heaven, we too will be given brand new bodies. There will be no more aching bones, no more sore muscles. As I grow older, I can only dream about the fresh energy — never again to feel weighed down and weary. I look forward to the day when the words in Isaiah 40 are our literal reality:

> *But they that wait upon the LORD shall renew their strength; they shall mount up with wings as eagles; they shall run,*

*and not be weary; and they shall walk,
and not faint.*

Isaiah 40:31

There will be far more to these bodies than feeling forever young, of course. I want to take a glimpse into the nature of the glorified bodies we'll receive when our time on the earth is through. Remember, God makes snapdragons and daisies from dead seeds. We find a couple of different statements about what we will see. I want to focus on Paul in 1 Corinthians 15 as he answers those who are skeptical of the resurrection of the dead. He says:

But some man will say, How are the dead raised up? and with what body do they come? Thou fool, that which thou sowest is not quickened, except it die: And that which thou sowest, thou sowest not that body that shall be, but bare grain, it may chance of wheat, or of some other grain: But God giveth it a body as it hath pleased him, and to every seed his own body.

1 Corinthians 15:35-38

In other words, we throw seed out in a field, but the seed of grain is nothing like the whole plant. There's a significant, obvious difference between the hard-shelled little sunflower seed and the big, bright and cheery sunflower. The tiny gray poppy seed bears no resemblance to the lovely red and orange blossoms of the poppy flower. Paul notes that God has given every kind of seed its own unique plant body. Paul then takes a little walk through some basic natural history, describing the variety of God's creation:

> *All flesh is not the same flesh: but there is one kind of flesh of men, another flesh of beasts, another of fishes, and another of birds. There are also celestial bodies, and bodies terrestrial: but the glory of the celestial is one, and the glory of the terrestrial is another. There is one glory of the sun, and another glory of the moon, and another glory of the stars: for one star differeth from another star in glory.*
> 1 Corinthians 15:39-41

He is clearly leading up to something, because his whole point is to explain the resurrection of the dead. Our flesh is currently a terrestrial flesh, but it does have a glory. Anybody who studies biology recognizes the amazing work of art that is the living cell. This dying shell we have right now is nothing to sniff at. We can watch the Olympics and sit amazed at the feats that can be accomplished by the human body. Even then, we won't always have a terrestrial body. We will be given a body with no genetic defects, no weaknesses. It will be body of a much greater glory, designed to last forever.

> *So also is the resurrection of the dead.*
> *It is sown in corruption; it is raised in*
> *incorruption: It is sown in dishonour; it is*
> *raised in glory: it is sown in weakness; it is*
> *raised in power: It is sown a natural body;*
> *it is raised a spiritual body. There is a*
> *natural body, and there is a spiritual body.*
> 1 Corinthians 15:42-44

Now, pay attention to what Paul does. This is the best part.

> *And so it is written, The first man Adam*
> *was made a living soul; the last Adam*
> *was made a quickening spirit. Howbeit*
> *that was not first which is spiritual, but*
> *that which is natural; and afterward that*
> *which is spiritual. The first man is of the*
> *earth, earthy: the second man is the Lord*
> *from heaven. As is the earthy, such are they*
> *also that are earthy: and as is the heavenly,*
> *such are they also that are heavenly. And as*
> *we have borne the image of the earthy, we*
> *shall also bear the image of the heavenly.*
> 1 Corinthians 15:45-49

That should make us jump for joy. Adam failed. We have lived our whole lives bearing his earthy, broken image. This body can do remarkable things, but in the end, it's made of clay. There will be a day, though, when we can cast off this clay shell and bear the image of Christ in all His strength and eternal power and glory. That is amazing.

The disciples were obviously not able to see Jesus in His full heavenly form after He rose from the dead. Yet, even then, He provided clues that there was far more to Him than meets the eye.

Walking Through Walls

In John 20:19, we find the disciples hiding away from the Jewish authorities. The room where they are hiding has four walls and a floor and a ceiling, and they've locked the doors tight because they are terrified. Just three days prior, they had watched Jesus whipped and brutally tormented and executed. Jesus had warned them that these things would happen and that He would rise again, but His words hadn't made sense to them. Suddenly, that Sunday evening the Lord appears in the middle of them.

Jesus greets them and says, "Peace be unto you." He makes it clear to them that He's not a ghost. He shows them the scars in His hands and feet to prove his identity and to calm them down. "Behold my hands and my feet," He says in Luke 24:39, "that it is I myself: handle me, and see; for a spirit hath not flesh and bones, as ye see me have." He is tangible. He is not a holographic projection. "Handle me and see." He wants to prove to them that He is physical and real and alive. He asks for some food, and they give him fish and honeycomb, and He eats it. I find it interesting that Jesus never appeared after His death without eating. He's my kind of guy.

Jesus went through steps to demonstrate to His disciples that He was tangible, yet it doesn't escape our notice that He was able to enter that room *without walking through a door!* He just appeared before them. It was the same a few verses earlier in Luke 24. He was in Emmaus, sitting down to a meal with two men. He broke bread with them, and then He simply vanished.

Jesus performed no appearing and disappearing acts before His death and resurrection. He walked on water, but He walked from the shore to get there. After His resurrection, He repeatedly showed up in rooms without using the door. That tells us something. It tells us that He had gained the ability to move about in more than our basic three spatial dimensions. He did it again the next week, this time when Thomas the doubter was present.

> *And after eight days again his disciples were within, and Thomas with them: then came Jesus, the doors being shut, and stood in the midst, and said, Peace be unto you. Then saith he to Thomas, Reach hither thy finger, and behold my hands; and reach hither thy hand, and thrust it into my side: and be not faithless, but believing.*
>
> John 20:26-27

John makes a point to note that the doors were shut. Jesus was not a smoke and mirrors illusionist. There were no trap doors hidden by a dry ice mist. He simply appeared, and Thomas was able to touch and feel Him and be satisfied.

We do know that our bodies are going to have more than three spatial dimensions. There is a term that appears only twice in the Bible, but it's important. The Greek word *oikētērion* (οἰκητήριον) refers to the dwelling place for the spirit. It's this holy body, this "habitation" that the fallen angels left behind in Jude 1:6-7. It is also the word used in 2 Corinthians 5:2 to describe the bodies we will have. The King James translates it as "our house" when we are resurrected: "For in this we groan, earnestly desiring to be clothed upon with our house which is from heaven:"

Remember the Transfiguration in Matthew 17 and Luke 9, when Jesus went up on the mountain with Peter, James and John to pray. Jesus was transformed before them.

> *And as he prayed, the fashion of his countenance was altered, and his raiment was white and glistering. And, behold, there talked with him two men, which were Moses and Elias: Who appeared in glory, and spake of his decease which he should accomplish at Jerusalem.*
>
> Luke 9:29-31

This is a mysterious moment in the Lord's history on earth. He glowed with God's glory there on the mountain. What's perhaps more interesting is that the three disciples were able to see Moses and Elijah in their glorified forms, and the disciples *recognized* Moses and Elijah.

I don't think we have the capacity to understand the full nature of our resurrected bodies from our perspective right now. It's like trying to understand a tiger from a two-dimensional drawing of one paw print. It's even worse than that if M Theory is correct and the full reality has 10 dimensions.

Whatever the case, when we are with God, we will finally be able to comprehend Him because we will be in the same dimensionality as He is. This is the wonder that we find in 1 John 3:2:

> *Beloved, now are we the sons of God, and it doth not yet appear what we shall be: but we know that, when he shall appear, we shall be like him; for we shall see him as he is.*

We will no longer see reality as a two-dimensional representation of a multi-dimensional being. We'll no longer see the pencil sketch version. We'll be able to experience the full and whole greater reality. We will see Him as He is, because we will be like Him. Whatever dimensionality He enjoys, so shall we. That's what this is saying. Wow. That's exciting.

Chapter 12
Heaven and the New Jerusalem

All our common media images of Heaven seem to me incredibly disappointing. If I thought that we would be sitting all day on clouds playing harps, I would think Heaven was the most boring place in the world. This is an area we truly need to toss away our presuppositions and get as close to understanding the truth as we can within our limited perspective.

I want you to think about something for just a moment. This world we live in right now is gorgeous and varied and dynamic. We find rainforests with moss so thick on the tree trunks that we can lay back and sink into it. We find fantastic fish and anemones and other colorful sea creatures under the water just off tropical coasts. The world is fun to explore because there are mountains, prairies, savannas, and vast canyons, each with its own system of living creatures. The whole world is amazing, and we all know it.

Yet, this world is doomed to die. It's our current home, and we need to keep our house clean and maintained. God made this world with the foreknowledge that it was going to be destroyed one day. I cannot imagine the glories of the world He has created to last forever. To suggest for a second that Heaven will be boring completely underestimates God's creative brilliance in the face of the ingenuity we see all around us.

What will Heaven really be like? We only get a brief picture of the heavenly kingdom in Revelation. We get just the smallest glimpse, but we can glean some things from it.

We see that there is a river of living water flowing from the throne of God, and beside the river the Tree of Life is growing. Not only is it a tree, but it's the Tree of Life, and not only is it a fruit tree, but it bears twelve different kinds of fruits. That tells us that God has changed things up a few notches.

> *And he shewed me a pure river of water of life, clear as crystal, proceeding out of the throne of God and of the Lamb. In the midst of the street of it, and on either side of the river, was there the tree of life, which bare twelve manner of fruits, and yielded her fruit every month: and the leaves of the tree were for the healing of the nations.*
>
> Revelation 22:1-2

This is one of the reasons I believe that Adam and Eve enjoyed living in higher dimensions before they sinned and were kicked out of the Garden of Eden. Here we find the Tree of Life, alive and well, growing beside the river of life that flows from God's throne. Adam and Eve once had a one-on-one personal relationship with God, and they lost that. I suspect they lost the ability to see and enjoy the spiritual world. I think all of human reality was torn at the Fall, and our first parents were relegated to a living experience within the four-dimensional framework of space-time.

At any rate, the Tree of Life is there in paradise with God, and it bears its fruits anew every month — twelve different kinds of fruits. That's fun! Will there be eating in Heaven? You bet! There will be eating, and there will be drinking. We will be able to drink from the river of life:

> *And he said unto me, It is done. I am Alpha and Omega, the beginning and the end. I will give unto him that is athirst of the fountain of the water of life freely.*
>
> Revelation 21:6

I doubt that the Tree of Life is the only source of food. Remember, the very first thing we do in Christ's eternal kingdom is attend the marriage supper of the Lamb!

Marriage Supper

> *Let us be glad and rejoice, and give honour to him: for the marriage of the Lamb is come, and his wife hath made herself ready. And to her was granted that she should be arrayed in fine linen, clean and white: for the fine linen is the righteousness of saints. And he saith unto me, Write,*

Blessed are they which are called unto the marriage supper of the Lamb. And he saith unto me, These are the true sayings of God.
Revelation 19:7-9

Is the marriage supper of the Lamb an actual meal? I'm certain it is! Jesus makes several allusions to the wedding feast even when He is telling parables. He is going to go take His bride, the Church, and it will be a time of great rejoicing! He tells us:

The kingdom of heaven is like unto a certain king, which made a marriage for his son, And sent forth his servants to call them that were bidden to the wedding: and they would not come. Again, he sent forth other servants, saying, Tell them which are bidden, Behold, I have prepared my dinner: my oxen and my fatlings are killed, and all things are ready: come unto the marriage.
Matthew 22:2-4

In this parable, the people who were initially invited found excuses not to come, so the king sent his servants out into the highways to gather people to come to his feast. This is a picture of the Pharisees and Jewish leaders who rejected Christ, and many of us, Jews and Gentiles alike, are the beneficiaries of their negligence, because we've been bidden to the feast in their place.

We see several New Testament references to Jesus as a bridegroom coming to marry His bride.[36] We also see that Jesus was not only capable of eating after His resurrection, but He was always ready to eat something.[37] As I said, Jesus is my kind of guy.

The New Jerusalem

Of course, there is far more to the new heavens and earth than clouds and harps. In Revelation 21, we are offered a description of the heavenly city of New Jerusalem descending toward the New Earth. I suspect that John's human efforts to explain it fall far short, but he portrays it for us as well as he can. He tells us:

And he carried me away in the spirit to a great and high mountain, and shewed me that great city, the holy Jerusalem, descending out of heaven from God, Having the glory of God: and her light was like unto a stone most precious, even like a jasper stone, clear as crystal; And had a wall great and high, and had twelve gates, and at the gates twelve angels, and names written thereon, which are the names of the twelve tribes of the children of Israel: On the east three gates; on the north three gates; on the south three gates; and on the west three gates.

Revelation 21:10-13

Already, this is an impressive description. We have an enormous brilliant city, filled with light that shines as through a clear crystal. Imagine a city set with diamonds. Imagine how those gems catch the light and flash it everywhere. This is the city, prepared like a bride to meet her new husband. There are no Hollywood special effects. This city is more real than anything we've ever experienced — as though this present world has just been a dream, and we've woken to a new day.

Next, John gives us the dimensions of the city, and it is enormous.

> *And the wall of the city had twelve foundations, and in them the names of the twelve apostles of the Lamb. And he that talked with me had a golden reed to measure the city, and the gates thereof, and the wall thereof. And the city lieth foursquare, and the length is as large as the breadth: and he measured the city with the reed, twelve thousand furlongs. The length and the breadth and the height of it are equal.*

Revelation 21:14-16

The word translated "furlongs" here is the Greek word *stadia*. One stadion was equal to about 607 feet or 0.115 miles. In other words, this city is a cube that is 12,000 stadia — or 1380 miles — along each side. To appreciate the magnitude of this distance, this is about the same distance as the crow flies between Denver, Colorado and Washington, Pennsylvania, or between the northern border of Illinois to the Gulf of Mexico. This city is vast in its size. We cannot comprehend its vastness. What's more, it's a cube — as high as it is wide and long. The Hubble Space telescope orbits at just 380 miles above the surface of the planet. So, multiply that distance by 3.63, and we have the height of the New Jerusalem.

There are twelve gates into the city, three on each side, and on each gate is the name of one of the twelve tribes of Israel. There are twelve foundations for the city wall, and those foundations have the names of the twelve apostles. John gets a good look at the walls of the city. He describes them as pure gold, clear as glass, and the foundation stones are all manner of gemstones.

These are not just gemstones, they are the same stones the LORD ordered to be placed in the breastplate worn by Aaron, close to his heart, when he entered the Holy of Holies.[38] The breastplate was as long as it was wide, and each of the stones in the breastplate was associated with one of the names of the twelve tribes. We find that all the different parts of the Tabernacle represented the realities of objects in Heaven around the throne of God. The cherubim in the Tabernacle represented the actual cherubim who guard the throne of God. The Holy of Holies was His throne room on Earth. Here, we have an apparent connection between the stones in Aaron's breastplate and the foundation stones of the eternal city.

> *And I saw no temple therein: for the Lord God Almighty and the Lamb are the temple of it. And the city had no need of the sun, neither of the moon, to shine in it: for the glory of God did lighten it, and the Lamb is the light thereof. And the nations of them which are saved shall walk in the light of it: and the kings of the earth do bring their glory and honour into it. And the gates of it shall not be shut at all by day: for there shall be no night there.*

There is no more Temple. There will no longer be a need for inner rooms and candlesticks and showbread and breastplates. The toy models are gone, put away because the genuine articles have come to take their place. Even the sun that we have now is merely a placeholder for the much greater reality of God's own light. It's like trying to imagine the power and beauty of a thundering white Friesian horse, when crayon drawings of stick ponies are all we've ever known.

Some people have read the descriptions of the New Jerusalem and said, "That's impossible. This must not be a physical city on the earth." It's too large. It's too tall. They list a variety of problems and violations of the laws of physics as they are now — which of course is all nonsense. The New Earth is not the present earth. The city is clearly more than simply a three-dimensional cube. It's the residence of multi-dimensional beings — all who have been given upgraded bodies, and the glorified Christ Himself. I wouldn't even try to paint the New Jerusalem, because I believe John was trying to explain a city that exists in a far greater dimensionality that we can express on canvas.

The city is just the beginning. If the city alone is nearly 1400 miles on each side, then I suspect the rest of that new world will be unfathomable in size. This is the world created to last forever. Perhaps it goes on and on, and we'll never run out of new places to explore.

All these things are wonderful to think about. New bodies. A new world with endless possibilities. I believe that the beauty and excitement of these things are nothing, however, compared to the joy of being in the presence of the Most High God. All the years we struggled away from Him, unable to see, unable to hear, communicating with our Lord through prayers and visions and the words He's given to His prophets — all those years will be over. We will be able to see Him ourselves. We will be able to go straight up to Him and talk to Him face to face. We will be able to comprehend Him and enjoy Him in all His splendor, because we will be like He is.

> *And I heard a great voice out of heaven saying, Behold, the tabernacle of God is with men, and he will dwell with them,*

and they shall be his people, and God himself shall be with them, and be their God. And God shall wipe away all tears from their eyes; and there shall be no more death, neither sorrow, nor crying, neither shall there be any more pain: for the former things are passed away. And he that sat upon the throne said, Behold, I make all things new. And he said unto me, Write: for these words are true and faithful.

Revelation 21:3-5

Chapter 13
The Good News

As we come down to the end here, I want to be able to spend some time rejoicing. The great, holy God of the Universe made a way for us to be with Him forever. We have a future ahead of us that is bright and joyous. The Lord will wipe away all our tears, and we will dwell in His presence forever. That's exciting. We simply pray that our lives will be a blessing to the Lord who loves us. We pray that we can be His hands and arms in this world, holding and helping those who need to know Him — that we can be lights on a hill, leading as many people into His kingdom as will come.

Imagine that every one of us is guaranteed a trip to a foreign country for the rest of our lives. Let's say it's a given. Each and every person has the option of living out their lives at a pleasant south sea island — as peacefully remote as we desire. If we don't choose the pleasant tropical paradise, however, we'll be stuck in a gulag in Siberia. Let's say we all have a choice in the matter. We wouldn't want to leave our final destination to chance. We would want to make some efforts to ensure we had gotten our passports ready and had finalized our reservations at our location of choice. It would be dreadful to realize we'd had the option to live out our days with our favorite people, with mangos and lemon spritzers in our rooms, and dancing in the evening, but we ended up being screamed at in a prison in some frozen wasteland.

We have to go through the process of making sure our final destination is the pleasant one. We need to tell our children, "Get your reservations now. You never know when they'll call your name to catch your flight."

Yet, too many of us live our lives on this planet hardly cognizant that a future awaits us on the other side of the veil. Each and every one of us will cross a threshold into another adventure, and few of us have taken the trouble to investigate what's coming.

We are blessed, because we are recipients of the Gospel. It has not been hidden from us. What is the Gospel? What is that good news? The Gospel is something very specific. Near the end of his first epistle to the Corinthians, Paul gives the church a reminder saying:

> *Moreover, brethren, I declare unto you the gospel which I preached unto you, which also ye have received, and wherein ye stand; By which also ye are saved, if ye keep in memory what I preached unto you, unless ye have believed in vain…For I delivered unto you first of all that which I also received, how that Christ died for our sins according to the scriptures; And that*

he was buried, and that he rose again the third day according to the scriptures:
1 Corinthians 15:1-4

That's it. What's astonishing about this definition of the Gospel is that there's no mention of Christ's example. There's no mention of His teachings. Many people acknowledge that Jesus is the greatest teacher who ever lived. There's no mention of Jesus' miracles. Jesus warned us in Mark 13:22 that in the last times there would be false prophets and false Christs who would show signs and wonders. We cannot trust individuals simply because they are able to do miracles. There are wicked, deceptive spirits out there.

The Gospel is something very specific. It's this: Jesus died for our sins. He died visibly and publicly. He didn't simply vanish one day. He died, and He did so according to the Scriptures. A multitude of verses were fulfilled in the way that Jesus died. The cross was not a tragedy. Instead, it was the greatest achievement of all time. Through the cross, the Creator facilitated our redemption!

And you, being dead in your sins and the uncircumcision of your flesh, hath he quickened together with him, having forgiven you all trespasses; Blotting out the handwriting of ordinances that was against us, which was contrary to us, and took it out of the way, nailing it to his cross; And having spoiled principalities

and powers, he made a shew of them
openly, triumphing over them in it.
Colossians 2:13-15

Isn't that fantastic? He nailed our sins to the cross, and then He smashed to pieces the strongholds of those spiritual beings who hated Him, publicly humiliating them!

Next, Jesus was buried, which Paul emphasizes when he makes an analogy between Christ's burial and baptism.[39] Then, He rose — again according to the Scriptures — and a wide variety of people saw Him alive, including 500 brethren all at once.[40] Paul notes that most of those people "are still alive" (some of which might have been people at the Corinthian church). The point is that those individuals could be sought out for their own eyewitness reports.

All this is important, because Jesus Christ came to undo the damage done by Adam. Adam was the direct creation of God. The rest of us are descendants of Adam, and we carry in us a sin defect. When Jesus came as a human being, John 1:11-13 tells us He came unto His own, and those who receive Him are given the power to become the children of God. In Christ, we are no longer the descendants of Adam. We are born brand new. We are once again the direct creations of God, created in perfection just like Adam. That's why the term "born again" is not just a figure of speech. It's real.

Paul continues in 1 Corinthians 15 to explain the ultimate end of the whole matter:

But now is Christ risen from the dead, and become the firstfruits of them that slept. For since by man came death, by man came also the resurrection of the dead. For as in Adam all die, even so in Christ shall all be made alive.

1 Corinthians 15:20-22

When Jesus returns, He will bring to life all those who have died, so that we can live forever. At the end of time on this planet, Jesus Christ will once and for all destroy the evil powers that have plagued our world. Then finally, He will put an end to death itself:

But every man in his own order: Christ the firstfruits; afterward they that are Christ's at his coming. Then cometh the end, when he shall have delivered up the kingdom to God, even the Father; when he shall have put down all rule and all authority and power. For he must reign, till he hath put all enemies under his feet. The last enemy that shall be destroyed is death.

1 Corinthians 15:23-26

We will be able to shed this mortal coil one day. We will cast off this old, broken baggage and become the beautiful, powerful sons and daughters of God — made in His image as we were always meant to be.

> *So when this corruptible shall have put on incorruption, and this mortal shall have put on immortality, then shall be brought to pass the saying that is written, Death is swallowed up in victory. O death, where is thy sting? O grave, where is thy victory? The sting of death is sin; and the strength of sin is the law. But thanks be to God, which giveth us the victory through our Lord Jesus Christ.*
>
> 1 Corinthians 15:55-57

Our salvation was not an afterthought. God knew the plan all along, and even in the Garden after our first parents sinned, God began to show the human race how He planned to fix our problem. When Adam and Eve tried to cover themselves, God took away their pitiful leaves. Our efforts to cover our own sins always will end in failure. In the Garden, God the Father sacrificed an animal and presented its skins to Adam and Eve to cover them. God's plan of redemption has always been to slay His innocent Lamb, to shed His blood that we might be saved. It has been His plan since the beginning of the world.[41]

Mankind fell in a Garden, but on another tree in another garden, Jesus would take the place of our first father, and He would undo the power of the curse on our eternities. The self-sacrifice of

Jesus Christ gave God the opportunity to extend a complete pardon and to make us eligible for an eternal destiny.

We live on the timeline right now. The past is a memory, and the future is just a hope. None of us know when our last day will be, and our eternities are just a heartbeat away. A car accident, a stroke, a stray bullet could end our lives in a moment. Right now, each of us is either destined for everlasting life in Heaven or an everlasting punishment in Hell, depending on our position under Jesus Christ. He cares about us, but He only issues visas on this side of the border.

I often think there are people we will see in Heaven that we absolutely did not expect to see there, and there won't be people in Heaven we thought were doing great. God doesn't judge based on the outward appearances. He judges based on the heart. He sees us. He knows who we are, and every one of us should go cling to His hand like little children and say, "Wherever You're going, I want to go along too."

Father we praise You that there are no accidents in your kingdom, that every person who is reading or hearing these words is doing so by Your divine appointment. Precious Father, I pray they would have no peace until they can find their peace in You. As they seek You, I pray You would show them the way to find You. I pray that they discover the person of Jesus Christ and recognize the extremes You've gone to, that we might spend an eternity in Your presence.

Father, please give them a sense of their safety in You and the high value You have put on each one of them. Thank You for the amazing gift You have given us. Not just access to Heaven, but an eternity as Your own sons and daughters. Please forgive and cover our sins, and lead us by the hand. We trust You, Father, and we love You. We commit ourselves into Your capable hands without any reservation in the name of Jesus the Messiah, Your Son, our Lord and Savior and righteous Judge, amen.

Endnotes

1 - See our study *The Sovereignty of Man* for an in-depth analysis of what the Bible says about the balance between God's sovereignty and human responsibility.

2 - As quoted (or paraphrased) by William H. Poole in the 1879 book *The British Nation: The Lost Tribes of Israel.* The original is not to be found in William Paley's own works, but something similar is found in his 1794 book, *A View of the Evidences of Christianity.* This quote is often incorrectly attributed to Herbert Spenser.

3 - John 16:33

4 - Matthew 3:7; Luke 3:7

5 - Cf. Genesis 23:19, 25:9; 50:13

6 - Matthew 16:18

7 - Job 17:16

8 - 2 Peter 2:4

9 - Jeremiah 32:35

10 - Job 33:22-30

11 - I'm indebted to Gayle Erwin for showing me this poem at a men's conference.

12 - Hosea 4:6

13 - Deuteronomy 6:16; Luke 4:12

14 - Genesis 18:25; 1 Samuel 16:7; John 7:24; 2 Corinthians 10:7; 2 Timothy 4:8

15 - John 1:1-3; Colossians 1:16-17

16 - Carmichael, A. (1924, 2011) *Mimosa: A True Story*. Fort Washington, PA: CLC Publications.

17 - Isaiah 42:6; 49:6; Luke 2:32; Acts 26:23

18 - Isaiah 19:23-25

19 - I do not know the original source, but the story can be found in Hicks, L. and Jekel, B. (2006). *Better Bridges*. Pensacola, FL: A Beka Book.

20 - Romans 3:23, Ephesians 2:8-9

21 - Revelation 21:6, 22:13; Isaiah 55:8-9

22 - Ost, L. (2014, April 3). NIST Launches a New U.S. Time Standard: NIST-F2 Atomic Clock. Retrieved December 22, 2015, from http://www.nist.gov/pml/div688/nist-f2-atomic-clock-040314.cfm

23 - Witten, E. (1995). String Theory Dynamics in Various Dimensions. **

24 - Einstein, A; Podolsky, B; Rosen, N, (1935). Can Quantum-Mechanical Description of Physical Reality be Considered Complete?, *Physical Review* 47 (10): 777–780.

25 - Bell, J. (1964). On the Einstein-Podolsky-Rosen Paradox, *Physics* 1: 195–200

26 - Aspect, A., Dalibard, J., & Roger, G. (1982). Experimental Test of Bell's Inequalities Using Time-Varying Analyzers. *Physical Review Letters*, 49, 1804-1807.

27 - Davies, P., & Brown, J. (1986). John Bell. In *The ghost in the atom: A discussion of the mysteries of quantum physics* (p. 50). Cambridge: Cambridge University Press.

28 - Setterfield, B. (2007). Reviewing the Zero Point Energy. *Journal of Vectorial Relativity*, 2(3), 1-28.

29 - For example, see *Footprints of the Messiah, Daniel's 70 Weeks, The Feasts of Israel, Beyond Coincidence*, all available through http://resources.khouse.org. We also have many articles on these same subjects available for free at www.khouse.org.

Endnotes

30 - There is better evidence that Moses, Isaiah and Daniel all wrote the books credited to them. See our study *How We Got Our Bible* for a closer examination of the authorship of the Law of Moses and *How to Study the Bible* for an examination of the authorships of Isaiah and Daniel.

31 - Luke 23:43

32 - Leviticus 23:10-11; Matthew 28:1

33 - John 5:27; 2 Timothy 4:8

34 - Acts 3:19

35 - Romans 6:23

36 - Matthew 25:1-13; Mark 2:19-20; Luke 5:34-35, 22:16; John 3:29; 2 Corinthians 11:2; Ephesians 5:25-32

37 - Luke 24:30,41-43; John 21:9-14

38 - Exodus 28:15-21, 29-30

39 - Romans 6:2-5

40 - 1 Corinthians 15:6

41 - 1 Peter 1:20; Revelation 13:8

About the Author

Chuck Missler
Founder, Koinonia House

Chuck Missler was raised in Southern California.

Chuck demonstrated an aptitude for technical interests as a youth. He became a ham radio operator at age nine and started piloting airplanes as a teenager. While still in high school, Chuck built a digital computer in the family garage.

His plans to pursue a doctorate in electrical engineering at Stanford University were interrupted when he received a Congressional appointment to the United States Naval Academy at Annapolis. Graduating with honors, Chuck took his commission in the Air Force. After completing flight training, he met and married Nancy (who later founded The King's High Way Ministries). Chuck joined the Missile Program and eventually became Branch Chief of the Department of Guided Missiles.

Chuck made the transition from the military to the private sector when he became a systems engineer with TRW, a large aerospace firm. He then went on to serve as a senior analyst with a non-profit think tank where he conducted projects for the intelligence community and the Department of Defense. During that time, Chuck earned a master's degree in engineering at UCLA, supplementing previous graduate work in applied mathematics, advanced statistics and information sciences.

Recruited into senior management at the Ford Motor Company in Dearborn, Michigan, Chuck established the first international computer network in 1966. He left Ford to start his own company, a computer network firm that was subsequently acquired by Automatic Data Processing (listed on the New York Stock Exchange) to become its Network Services Division.

As Chuck notes, his day of reckoning came in the early '90s when — as the result of a merger — he found himself the chairman and a major shareholder of a small, publicly owned development company known as Phoenix Group International. The firm established an $8 billion joint venture with the Soviet Union to supply personal computers to their 143,000 schools. Due to several unforeseen circumstances, the venture failed. The Misslers lost everything, including their home, automobiles and insurance.

It was during this difficult time that Chuck turned to God and the Bible. As a child he had developed an intense interest in the Bible; studying it became a favorite pastime. In the 1970s, while still in the corporate world, Chuck began leading weekly Bible studies at the 30,000 member Calvary Chapel Costa Mesa, in California. He and Nancy established Koinonia House in 1973, an organization devoted to encouraging people to study the Bible.

Chuck had enjoyed a longtime, personal relationship with Hal Lindsey, who upon hearing of Chuck's professional misfortune, convinced him that he could easily succeed as an independent author and speaker. Over the years, Chuck had developed a loyal following. (Through Doug Wetmore, head of the tape ministry of Firefighters for Christ, Chuck learned that over 7 million copies of his taped Bible studies were scattered throughout the world.) Koinonia House then became Chuck's full-time profession.

Hidden Treasures

For the novice, as well as the sophisticate, this book is full of surprises. It includes subtle discoveries lying just "beneath" the text – hidden messages, encryptions, deliberate misspellings and other amendments to the text – that present implications beyond the immediate context, demonstrating a skillful design that has its origin from outside our space and time. Drawing upon over forty years of collecting, Chuck highlights in this book many of the precious nuggets that have become characteristic of his popular Bible studies around the world.

It is guaranteed to stimulate, provoke, and, hopefully, to disturb. It will confound the skeptic and encourage the believer. It is a "must read" for every thinking seeker of truth and serious inquirer of reality.

Other Resources

Learn the Bible

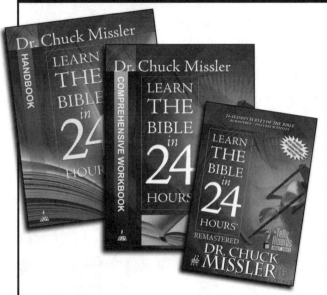

Are you ready for a detailed yet thoroughly enjoyable study of the most profound book ever written?

Using sound scientific facts, historical analysis, and Biblical narrative, acclaimed teacher Dr. Chuck Missler weaves together a rich tapestry of information—providing an accurate understanding of Scripture's relation to itself, to us and to the world at large.

Examine the heroic tales of Exodus, the lasting wisdom of Proverbs, or even the enigmatic imagery of Revelation with the simple, Scripturally sound insights and fresh perspectives found in *Learn the Bible in 24 Hours*. Whether you want to explore some of the less-discussed nuances of Scripture or you need a comprehensive refresher course on the Bible's themes and stories, *Learn the Bible in 24 Hours* is a great guide.

Available from https://Resources.khouse.org

How We Got Our Bible

- Where did our Bible come from? How good are the texts?
- Why do we believe its origin is supernatural?
- How do we know that it really is the Word of God?
- How accurate are our translations?
- Which version is the best?

Chuck Missler, an internationally recognized Biblical authority, reviews the origin of both the Old and New Testaments in light of recent discoveries and controversies.